EGYPT the Black Land

Series edited by Paul Johnstone *and* Anna Ritchie

Author and publishers join together in commending this book to the memory of the late Paul Johnstone.

EGYPT the Black Land

Paul
Jordan

PHAIDON·OXFORD

To my Father and Mother

I should like to express my gratitude to all those in Egypt
and Egyptology who over the years have helped and
guided me in the subject of this book: in particular,
Cyril Aldred of the Royal Scottish Museum who put my
native interest on a sounder basis and Frank Leek whose
criticism of my manuscript has proved so useful. I should
also like to acknowledge the debt I owe to the late Leslie
Greener in the matter of the history of Egyptology and to
the writings of Henri Frankfort on ancient Egyptian
religion. My thanks too to Mrs. Sally Kington who skil-
fully edited my manuscript and Mrs. June Broughton
who typed it. Needless to say, what errors may remain
belong entirely to the author.

Phaidon Press Limited, Littlegate House, St Ebbe's Street, Oxford
Published in the United States of America by E. P. Dutton & Co., Inc.

First published 1976

© 1976 Paul Jordan

ISBN: hardback   0 7148 1677 9
       paperback   0 7148 1722 8
Library of Congress Catalog Card Number: 76-5360

Filmset in Great Britain by BAS Printers Limited, Wallop, Hampshire

Printed in Italy by Amilcare Pizzi SpA, Milan

Contents

Chapter I   Napoleon in Egypt and Pre-Decipherment Mysteries — 7

Chapter II   The Land of Egypt and the First Egyptians — 26

Chapter III   Champollion's Decipherment and the Beginnings of Archaeology — 50

Chapter IV   Egyptian History in the Ancient World: to the End of the Old Kingdom — 74

Chapter V   Egyptian History in the Ancient World: to the Arab Conquest — 95

Chapter VI   Ancient Egyptian Society — 116

Chapter VII   Everyday Life and Life After Death — 135

Chapter VIII   The Technical and Scientific Achievements of Ancient Egypt — 151

Chapter IX   The Egyptian Outlook — 165

Chapter X   Egyptian Religion and Morality — 183

List of illustrations — 199

Index — 203

Napoleon sent this piece back to France as a present for Josephine: later William Randolph Hearst owned it.

Chapter I   Napoleon in Egypt and Pre-Decipherment Mysteries

On the first of July, 1798, a French army landed on the coast of Egypt near Alexandria. In command was a young man of twenty-nine years, who had persuaded the Republican government of France that Britain's grip on India might eventually be loosened by a French occupation of Egypt leading to direct communications between the Mediterranean and the Indian Ocean. This was seventy years before the opening of the Suez Canal, and the young Napoleon Bonaparte can have had only a very long-term eye on the strategic usefulness of Egypt to France.

He probably had a clearer view of the campaign's possibilities for enhancing his own fame and glory as his star rose in revolutionary France. Still, his ambitions were not merely military in character: perhaps for the first time since Caesar, here was a commander who took a real interest in the nature of the lands he set out to conquer. His army was not itself a large one, but with it went over one hundred and fifty scholars, scientists and artists who were to study, and report on, and illustrate the whole range of life in Egypt—its geology, its natural history, its people and its past. There was even a musician among the savants and the party was well equipped with all the books and scientific instruments that would be useful to their studies. It is interesting to note among the projects an intention to investigate plague and the eye-disease trachoma. One important piece of equipment was the printing press, for it was Napoleon's aim to bring Egypt at once into the community of readily-disseminated news and scholarship.

In encumbering his forces with this body of serious scholars, Napoleon was harnessing the aims of the late eighteenth century philosophers and scientists—especially the French Encyclopaedists, who wanted to rationalize all human knowledge—to his military adventure. Probably he realized that, scholars or not, they would have a tough time ahead of them: most of them were very young men. One of them wrote to his father before

7

setting out: 'It is established that a great number of scholars, the most distinguished in the various branches of knowledge, will be going on this voyage; and it seems equally certain that the expedition is to be accompanied by 25,000 troops. I forgot to tell you that some politicians claim that it is a question of cutting the Isthmus of Suez to establish communication between the Ocean and the Mediterranean.'

On the night of the first landings, the sea was very rough and a couple of dozen soldiers were drowned. The French landed without their big guns and without horses and set out to walk to Alexandria with Napoleon at their head. The Mamelukes, foreign mercenaries who ruled Egypt nominally for the Turkish Empire, wielded only medieval armies against them and, outnumbering the French greatly, completely underestimated the devastating impact of the fire-power of a modern European force on their romantic cavalry. Alexandria was quite unprepared when Bonaparte's slight forces moved against it on the morning of the 2nd of July and by noon the city was his. Napoleon's H.Q. for the assault on Alexandria was by Pompey's Pillar, a surviving monument from the Roman period of ancient Egypt. The scientists and artists went ashore on the 3rd and made their way to the H.Q. Napoleon's 'Commission of Arts and Science' was ready to start its studies alongside the soldiers in what was still only an imperfectly pacified town. They were not very well served by the general with special responsibility for them, who had other problems on his mind, and life was none too easy as they set about their labours. Bonaparte himself had taken up lodgings in the already established home of the French consul in Alexandria. Apparently enjoying his favour—he had been introduced by Josephine—was an aristocrat turned artist, named Vivant Denon. In the old days, Denon had catalogued Mme de Pompadour's jewels and been a favourite of Catherine of Russia and friend of Voltaire. He lost everything in the Revolution, but his skills at drawing (sometimes put to the service of high-class pornography) had found him a place in the new society. The mammoth many-volumed *Déscription de l'Egypte* is the just monument of the scholarly side of Napoleon's Egyptian adventure, but Denon's personal *Voyage in Upper and Lower Egypt* scooped it and remains a vivid account of the Commission's work.

Napoleon did not sit still in Alexandria and, by the end of July, 1798, Cairo had been captured. The Mamelukes had fared no better at the Battle of the Pyramids than they did at Alexandria—Napoleon took the occasion to harangue his men at the foot of the pyramids with an encouragement that has become famous: 'Soldiers, remember that from the top of these monuments forty centuries are looking down upon you!' This was a remarkably accurate assertion, for the time, since the chronology of the kings of ancient Egypt, whose pyramids they were, was far from firmly established before the late nineteenth century.

Pompey's Pillar, where
Napoleon set up his head-
quarters for his first assault
on Egypt, still stands in
Alexandria.

On the 1st of August the sea-battle of Abukir, the 'battle of the Nile', began. The consequences of Nelson's destruction of the French fleet in the Mediterranean now led Napoleon to encourage his forces in Egypt in new terms: 'You will all die like those brave men whose names are inscribed on the altars of fame, or you will return to your hearths, covered with honour and glory.' Apparently this blunt assessment did not go down very well with the troops. The French were quite cut off from home and the British were now enlisting Turkey's aid in ridding Egypt of them.

But the French were to stay in Egypt for three years and during that time to push right down south to the very borders of Egypt at Aswan. They were to do an enormous amount of scholarly work there, too. From the start, some of the Commission members had been sent off to Rosetta, a coastal town some 60 kilometres to the east of Alexandria. From there, some of them had seen the naval battle in Abukir Bay. Rosetta went on to become the most important single site of the French expedition's activities in Egypt.

In Cairo, meanwhile, although now without the support of French sea-power, Napoleon was pressing on with his plans. Five fine mansions had been taken over from their rich owners to house the 'Institute of Egypt'. Napoleon consented to be its first vice-president. This institute was to embody the practical achievements of the Commission of Arts and Science. Its early days were not all that peaceful, for in October an Arab uprising, with mobs attacking Frenchmen in the street and in their houses, led to the Institute's guard being withdrawn for urgent duties elsewhere. The scholars decided to defend their Institute themselves but, perhaps fortunately, it had not been attacked by the time the revolt was put down.

As the French came into firm control of more and more of the country, the scope for the work of the savants went on growing. The pyramids were partly explored (though many a European traveller had strayed in there in the preceding centuries) and work began to clear away the sand that had swamped the Sphinx up to its neck over the years. This sand clearing is not a once-and-for-all operation—the desert is continually blowing in and threatening to rebury the Sphinx's body. The French soldiery has been seriously maligned over the Sphinx. It is a common accusation that they are to blame for its dog-eared appearance at the present time on account of some high-spirited target practice during Napoleon's campaign. In fact, an Arab sheik of the fourteenth century had long-since done the damage when the French arrived and his reasons were pious ones to do with distaste for a pagan idol.

As the French forces pushed upstream into what we call 'Upper Egypt', the part of the country away from the Nile Delta and the Mediterranean ('Lower Egypt') and nearer to the equator in the south, the scholars

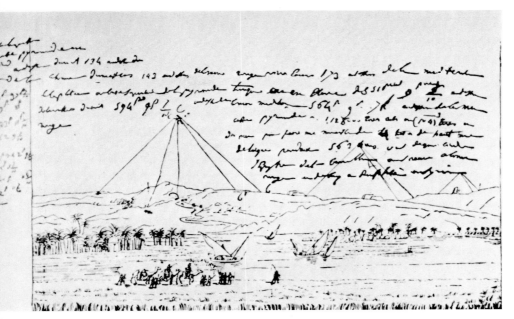

Above *Napoleon's own notes include sketches of the pyramids at Giza.*

Below *When Napoleon arrived at Giza, the Sphinx was buried up to its neck in sand.*

and artists went with them. At 9 am on the 26th of January, 1799, they arrived before Thebes and, soldiers and scholars alike, were arrested by the grandeur of its pillars and pylons and its reminders of Homer's 'hundred-gated' epithet. Vivant Denon wrote: 'One has to rub his eyes to be sure he is not in a dream.' It is well to remember that, all this time, these adventurous Frenchmen were cut off from all means of going home. Of the temple at Dendera, Denon wrote: 'What uninterrupted power, what wealth, what abundance, what superfluity of resources must have belonged to a government that could raise an edifice like this.' That sort of reaction was, and is, a common one in the face of Egyptian monumentality. Today there are those who even ask whether some super-power from outer space might not be needed to explain the ancient Egyptian achievement. Actually, Dendera is mostly a late work, from Greek and Roman times, and represents a considerable falling-off in the true Egyptian artistic tradition: Roman emperors even made additions to it.

In their travels in Egypt, the Frenchmen saw some fine things that simply do not exist today, like the temple of Armant still standing before all but its foundations were taken away to build a sugar factory. And so the work of the 'Commission of Arts and Science' went on mapping, collecting and drawing: not simply the antiquities of Egypt but many other of its aspects: of geography, natural history, ethnology and so on.

It was not, in fact, a member of the Commission who made the greatest contribution to its whole study. It was an officer of the Engineers named Pierre Bouchard. Napoleon was well aware that sea-communications with France would have to be restored and his own occupation of Egypt protected from British sea-power in the Mediterranean if the whole adventure was to thrive. The defences of the Mediterranean coast had therefore to be strengthened. Pierre Bouchard was working on an extension of Fort Julien (named after a French general) at Rosetta when a discovery was made whose importance he was fortunately able to recognize. The Engineers have always been known for their 'savvy' and, no doubt, the presence of the Commission had interested everyone in the other-than-military possibilities of the expedition. Bouchard, at all events, saw that something of great importance had turned up. Thanks to Napoleon's printing presses in Cairo, all Egypt—and soon France too, for scholarly communications could still slip through—was able to read in the 'Courier d'Egypte' for August, 1799, a letter from Pierre Bouchard, telling that he had found 'a stone of very fine granite, black, with a close grain, and very hard . . . with three distinct inscriptions separated in three parallel bands.' The important thing was that the bottom inscription was in readable Greek and the top one in those striking signs found all over Egyptian monuments and still, at that time, quite undecipherable— to the great frustration of all the scholars who wanted to get beyond the scraps of information the Greek and Latin authors could retail about

The Rosetta Stone was the prime clue to the decipherment of the ancient Egyptian writings. Names enclosed in 'cartouches' in the top register are elucidated on pages 56–58.

ancient Egypt. Indeed, so mysterious had these signs seemed from time to time, that the name of 'holy carvings' or 'hieroglyphs' had been put upon them. Now it was reasonable to assume that the hieroglyphs and the Greek on the stone from Rosetta, together with the other section of some sort of ancient Egyptian writing, might all mean the same thing, rather in the manner of a modern foreign-language phrase book with parallel bits of English and French or German. The 'Courier d'Egypte' permitted itself to observe: 'perhaps it will even give us the key at last.' This damaged basalt relic, with its three separated inscriptions, about the size of a small gravestone, became a hot property as soon as it was found. It was sent to Cairo where on Napoleon's orders it was carefully copied and where casts of it were made. Copies were soon in France. Translation of the Greek section confirmed that the text, a decree of 196 BC, was indeed a parallel two-language one. The decree was issued by Ptolemy V, a ruler of the Greek Period in Egypt, and the Rosetta Stone itself tells us that the same message was to be inscribed in both the Greek and Egyptian languages.

Napoleon himself left for home on the 19th of August, 1799, leaving his blockaded army in Egypt to its own devices. He had to go carefully, avoiding British patrols in the Mediterranean. In his baggage, among several other presents for Josephine, was a seated Egyptian statue that has had an interesting subsequent history. An English lord bought it in France in the last century, and in the Twenties it was snapped up by William Randolph Hearst, the American press baron: it is now in the Brooklyn Museum.

With Napoleon gone and the British fleet still watching over Alexandria, to say nothing of the menaces of the Turks, the new C.-in-C., General Kléber, set himself to arrange free passage with the British for the Commission to return to France. But back in France, Napoleon declared himself consul and this alteration in the government caused the British to delay the Commission's exit from Alexandria. The members of the Commission waited for a month at Rosetta and then for another month on board the 'Oiseau' while Sir Sydney Smith conferred with London. And then the situation changed again: under Kléber the French forces put forty thousand Turks to flight at the Battle of Heliopolis near Cairo, and the French were once more in control of Egypt. With this improvement in their affairs, some of the Commission members actually returned to Cairo. Then a muslim zealot assassinated Kléber in June of 1800 and in the following March the British landed at Abukir. The French were pushed back into Alexandria and the British were able to take Rosetta at the beginning of April. By midsummer, the English, the Turks and the Mamelukes were at the gates of Cairo, while the French inside were suffering from a water shortage and from plague. When the French sensibly gave in, the Commission members there were allowed to go back to Alexandria where the French were still holding out, eating their horses and camels. The Commission was in fact put back on board the 'Oiseau' but the new French C.-in-C., General Menou—a man of misguided talents who was determined to hold on to Egypt at all costs and had even gone Muslim in the hopes of speeding up Egypt's incorporation into 'La Patrie'—could not bring himself to arrange a safe-conduct for them with the English. So they left on the 10th of July, 1801, without one. Almost immediately, the 'Cynthia' put a shot across their bows. They kept on but signalled for a parley. They were taken into Abukir and their captain, with the mathematician Fourier, went on board Admiral Keith's 'Foud-royant'. The admiral declined to let them through because the French general had not obtained permission from him. There now began a farcical to-ing and fro-ing which took the 'Oiseau' twice back into Alexandria to General Menou with all the Commission members on board, their collections and notes and drawings. The first time, Menou threatened to sink them for parleying with the British instead of fighting, and they sailed out again. Before the 'Cynthia' saw them back a second time, some of the scholars had jumped into—or missed jumping into—Sir Sydney Smith's pinnace while he was on board for more negotiations. After this, Menou had to take them back into Alexandria. But evidently he had had some change of heart, for he finally surrendered the town on the 30th of August, 1801.

One of the terms of surrender was that the British should inherit all the Commission's collections of antiquities and natural history and whatever that they had found in Egypt. The French scholars would not accept this hard condition: they threatened to dump the entire product of their labours sooner than lose any of it to the British at this stage. The British were willing to discuss the matter as far as any of the material went, with the exception of the Rosetta Stone. They must have that. And there were two men on the British side who were absolutely determined to have as much French loot as they could. They were the civilian Daniel Clarke, much interested in all things Egyptian, who went on to write a travel book about Egypt and an account of the British army's exploits there, and William Hamilton, acting for Lord Elgin, similarly occupied in sophisticated looting in Greece. Clarke and Hamilton stole a good deal away from the French army, who had stolen it from the Egyptians, including a great sarcophagus hidden by the French on board a hospital ship. And Clarke knew only too well the value of the Rosetta Stone.

But the Stone was being kept in Menou's house in Alexandria, after being brought back from Cairo, and Menou wouldn't let it go. A young British colonel, Thomas Turner, took a party of soldiers by night and seized it. But not, of course, before the French had sent away copies and casts to Paris—indeed the Greek part of the inscription was now widely translated. Turner accompanied the Stone all the way back to England

15

to watch over its safety. There the Society of Antiquaries took possession of it at first and circulated copies of it through the non-French-speaking world. And then the Rosetta Stone passed to the British Museum, where its acquisition—along with other Egyptian antiquities—obliged Parliament to provide for the enlargement of the premises.

Back again in France, the French went on to produce their magnificent nineteen-volume, state-published 'Déscription de l'Egypte', which came out between 1809 and 1828. It has been calculated that by 1806 nearly a quarter of the young savants of the Commission were dead: five in battle, five by assassination, ten of plague, five of dysentery, one by drowning and five expiring back in Europe, exhausted by their Egyptian experience. Napoleon Bonaparte and Vivant Denon were elected honorary members of the newly formed American Academy of Arts for their work in opening up Egypt to scholarship. The success of the scholarly enterprise and of the 'Déscription' led to the steady publishing of more and more of the temple inscriptions and papyrus writings that the Commission had copied. The still unreadable written legacy of ancient Egypt was gaining currency. But it remained an awful mystery and drew a veil of obscurity over all efforts to understand more about the ancient Egyptian civilization than the classical authors had, perhaps inaccurately, handed down. The Rosetta Stone consequently endures as the most important single contribution among all the enterprising investigations inspired by Napoleon in Egypt: by virtue of its having afforded the means whereby the brilliant mind of Jean-François Champollion could crack the hieroglyphic 'code' and translate the ancient texts and inscriptions and dispel the clouds of mystery that obscured the lives of the ancient Egyptians until they could speak to us directly in their own words.

Just how mysterious the ancient Egyptians seemed before Champollion made it possible for them to speak for themselves in their own words, can be gauged from Lepidus's mistaken observations in 'Antony and Cleopatra': 'Your serpent of Egypt is bred now of your mud by the operation of your sun. So is your crocodile.' Shakespeare even put a window in a pyramid, relying too far on inaccurate travel accounts of his time. Still, travel accounts by European visitors to Egypt constituted probably the best pre-decipherment guide to the true nature of the ancient Egyptian civilization. What else had anyone to go on before the nineteenth century? The surest source of information was naturally taken to be the Bible: nearly everyone who wrote on matters touching history relied on the Bible as certain fact and tried to fit everything else into its account. So the adventures of, for example, Joseph and Moses in Egypt were fixed points about which all other conjectures had to circle. Perhaps the Bible is to blame, in the scene where Moses and Aaron struggle with pharaoh's magicians, for the undying conviction that the ancient Egyptians were great sorcerers and workers of magic. Second only to the Bible and

16

frequently regarded as equally 'gospel' truth, were the classical authors: among these, Herodotus, Greek writer of the fifth century BC, was the principal source of information.

Solon, the law-giver of Athens, had visited Egypt before him, but Herodotus was the first classical author to write a detailed account of what he had seen and heard there, in the middle of the fifth century BC. The cautionary thing to remember in his case is that, despite his having been dubbed the 'Father of History', he sometimes behaved like a modern tourist out at Giza who believes everything his 10-piastre guide tells him. Not all of Herodotus' Egyptian advisers can have known what they were talking about, or been in earnest if they did. In a sense, the latter-day Egyptians could not help but be the historians and even the archaeologists of their own civilization. The pyramids of Giza were two thousand years old when Herodotus saw them, a thousand years old in Tutankhamun's time—a longer span than separates us from the doings of king John. That favourite ancient Egyptian practice of tomb-robbing, which had almost certainly already cleaned out the pyramids in the time of Herodotus, is itself a form of archaeological investigation. Nevertheless, Egyptian history was still living history, with a continuity from the earliest days, when Herodotus was there, despite the periods of upheavel that had occurred and despite the Persians who were currently in control of the country. An indication of this historical continuity of Egyptian life is afforded at the temple associated with the collapsed pyramid of Meidum: Egyptian visitors of the Eighteenth Dynasty, in about 1600 BC, who came and scribbled on its walls still knew that it had belonged to king Snofru of the Fourth Dynasty, some thousand years earlier.

Herodotus travelled the length of the country, as far as Aswan at the Nubian border, and wrote vivid accounts of life along the Nile. He coined the apt characterization of Egypt as 'the gift of the Nile'. He had even heard of the notion that the life-bringing Nile rises and falls each year because of rains in the distant mountains of Africa. He is a witness to the fact that the Great Pyramid still wore its finely finished casing-stones in his day, before they were taken away some fifteen hundred years later to build the Arab city of Cairo. On the other hand, he credulously tells us that there is an artificial lake under the pyramids and he does not mention the Sphinx at all!

Subsequent classical travel writers are responsible for the colourful confusion of ancient Egypt with the Homeric World of the Iliad and Odyssey. When Greek and Roman travellers encountered the two colossal seated statues of the pharaoh Amenophis III at Thebes, they dubbed them the 'Colossi of Memnon' after the divinely-born Homeric hero who went to Priam's aid at Troy. One of these statues was famous in Roman times for singing in the morning sun—perhaps as the result of the escape of heated air as the day came on. It never sang again after about AD 200 when the Roman emperor Severus carried out a little restoration work upon it. The 'Labyrinth' by the pyramid of Hawara, about 100 kilometres to the south of Cairo, was so-called because its intricate complex of mortuary temples reminded Greek travellers of Daedalus' adventures on Crete in the palace of king Minos. Homer's epithet 'hundred-gated' for Thebes led to the use of the Greek name for the whole site of many-pyloned temples dotted around what are now the Arab villages of Luxor and Karnak. The ancient Egyptians called this area 'Weset' among other things—another of their names Tahut-Ipet resembled the Greek name 'Thebes'. Thebes is currently the name for the whole spread of temples and tombs, including the Valley of the Kings, on both banks of the Nile at Luxor.

In some ways, the classical ruling-class of latter-day ancient Egypt inevitably resembled the colonial rulers of the various nineteenth century empires of western Europe. As it happens their accounts of the country and its ways are less adequate than, say, a British civil servant's reminiscences of India. They never developed the study of anthropology that arose in the European imperial powers. Worse still they seem never to have bothered much with the language of the Egyptians or the various ways of writing it.

It is unfortunate then that the history of Egypt written in Greek in the time of Ptolemy II by a native Egyptian named Manetho—the most important classical work on the subject—did not survive into the European renaissance. It is given in excerpt together with its king-list (very useful in establishing a chronology for ancient Egypt) by the Romanized Jewish historian Josephus, and the pre-decipherment European scholars had to be content with that. Some of their other classical sources were not simply sketchy and inadequate, they were downright misleading: like Horapollon's assertion (he was writing in Greek in the fourth century AD) that the hieroglyphs were a purely symbolic form designed to express in an arcane way, and only to priestly initiates, the unfathomable mysteries of the ancient Egyptian religion. This version of what the hieroglyphs were all about, when Horapollon's work was re-discovered in the fifteenth century AD, put European scholars on the wrong track for centuries.

The pre-decipherment scholars could not, of course, make use of the ancient Egyptians' own account of themselves. But, in any case, the last of the ancient Egyptians had not been concerned to leave any heritage of their great days behind them. The Roman Empire had exploited Egypt very comprehensively, bleeding it into a ruinous state for its agricultural and mineral wealth. A taste for otherworldliness, created by the growing unpleasantness of everyday life, made Egypt vulnerable to Christianity years before Theodosius imposed it by decree on the fading Roman Empire at the end of the fourth century AD. The most otherworldly form of Christianity—monasticism—was developed in Egypt. The old gods

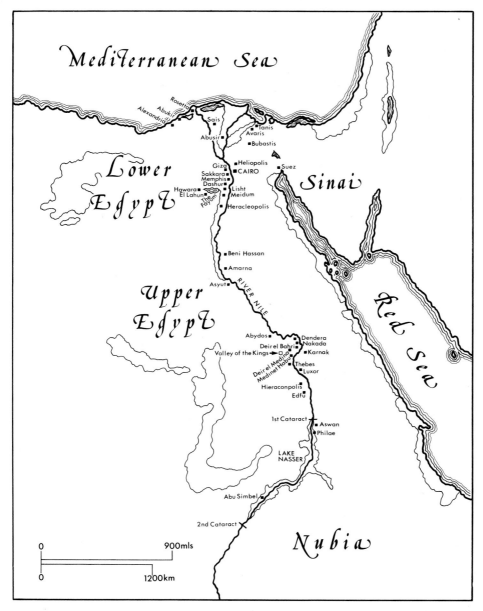

The principal sites of ancient Egypt.

were abandoned along with the impossibility of continuing to live in the old ways. Christian monks closed the last of the old temples and destroyed what they could of the pagan ancient Egyptian heritage. The first monks were probably the last Egyptians who could read hieroglyphs and they were concerned *not* to pass on their knowledge. They might speak their Coptic tongue (a direct evolution out of the ancient Egyptian language) but they wrote it in a modified Greek alphabet.

Everywhere the ancient temples were scorned, defaced or simply used for the convenience of the new way of life. The Luxor and Edfu temples, for example, became villages, with their new mud-brick houses propped up by the massive masonry of the past. Other ancient piles were robbed for building material. Ancient shrines were disfigured and altered to new purposes: a former three-figure statue group at Karnak has been ingeniously transformed into a cross by hacking away all of the two divine figures flanking the king except for the bits of their chests that extend his arms into a crucifixion.

The temple on the island of Philae in the Nile south of Aswan remained in the hands of the priests of the old religion longer than any other: it is a temple dedicated to Isis, the Egyptian goddess who had become a major Roman deity. The decree of Theodosius found the local inhabitants in Upper Egypt and Nubia still dedicated to their own mother-goddess, and it was left to Justinian in the middle of the sixth century AD finally to close Philae; its fabric survived so well because it was built on an island and could not easily be got at for purposes of robbery. It has been subject to flooding in recent times but will soon be magnificently restored to undunked splendour by the efforts of Unesco and the Egyptian Government.

The Arab conquest of AD 640–641 found a Christian Egypt that had already rejected and suppressed its own past, in accordance with Ezekiel's projection: 'Thebes shall be split asunder, and Memphis reduced to gravel'. In the last days of Roman Egypt the tourist could still go inside parts of the Great Pyramid—five hundred years later Mamun, son of Harun al-Rashid, had to force his way in, for the entrance was, by then, blocked with rubble. It is unlikely in the extreme that anything of Cheops' burial was left inside: that must have been robbed away in the days of the pharaohs, if it had ever been installed in the first place, something of which we cannot be quite sure. The Arabs were, however, generally concerned about the treasure potential of ancient tombs. The story of Aladdin and the great treasure behind the magically opened door goes back to tomb-robbing tales: the treasure is the funerary equipment of the dead man and the magically opened door is the 'false door' of the tomb inscribed with mysterious hieroglyphs. 'False doors' were imitations of real entrances set up as the scene of ritual offerings to the dead at ancient Egyptian tombs.

Above *The pyramids in their original state were faced with polished stone to shine in the sun: the top courses of Chephren's pyramid still carry their fine finish.*

Left *'False doors' were dummy entrances to some Egyptian tombs, mimicking the appearance of the working doorway of an Egyptian house.*

The Arabs went on to rob the Great Pyramid of all its fine casing-stones and the neighbouring Chephren Pyramid of nearly all of them (though at the top the remaining courses still shine a little in the sun). These stones were taken away for the building of the new city of Cairo in the thirteenth century AD. But, already, looting on a more-than-everyday scale had been carried out in Egypt: the Romans had made off with some large monuments, like the 30 metre high Lateran Obelisk in Rome which took the labours of two pharaohs, two emperors and a pope to put it finally where it is today; and when Justinian closed down the Philae temple he took some of its statues away to Constantinople.

The homes and everyday places of the ancient Egyptians, even their palaces, were built out of mud-brick and not out of 'eternal' stone like their temples and tombs. Preponderantly, it is the tombs and temples which have survived, lending a religiously weighted and even morbid air to the whole of this ancient civilization, while their homes and work places have crumbled away. A further imbalance in the survival of ancient Egyptian sites has a geographical character: above old Memphis, near to modern Cairo, in Upper Egypt (that is, the southern part of the country), where conditions are hot and dry and the distinction between river and cultivated land on the one hand and desert on the other is very clear, sites have survived very well; but in Lower Egypt, where the Delta fans out just north of Cairo to meet the Mediterranean in a multitude of streams, sites have vanished altogether, submersed beneath the water-table and largely disintegrated by the action of water and soil-agents. Memphis itself has nearly disappeared and it must always be remembered that the Lower Egypt of the Delta, about which less is known and heard, was as important a part of the country as Upper Egypt.

A doctor from Bagdad, named Abdel Latif, is one of our few witnesses to the state of affairs in Egypt in the thirteenth century AD when ancient buildings were being looted to build new ones. In his day, the Great Pyramid was not much touched and the Sphinx was undamaged. At this time, apart from the odd European traveller on his way to see the Christian Holy places, Egypt's only commerce with the West was occasioned by the European pseudo-medical conviction that 'mummy' was good for wounds and bruises. Originally, momia or mummiya meant mineral pitch or bitumen—which would have had some slight medical application. It came to refer to a mixture of pitch and myrrh, and specifically to the resinous traces that might be found in the embalmed bodies of ancient Egyptians. Soon it meant simply bits of the dried-up flesh of these bodies, and hence our word 'mummy'. In powdered form, it became a staple of the medieval apothecaries. Abdel Latif observed that, even when bitumenized fragments were concerned, 'mummy' could be no more efficaceous than real mineral pitch, and one Western commentator on the trade remarked drily: 'Pharaoh is sold for Balsams'. John Sanderson, an agent in Egypt for the Turkey Company (Turkey had taken control of Egypt in 1517) shipped about 250 kilos of it back to Europe between 1585 and 1587. Soon after that, the demand became so great that—largely in the hands of foreign merchants—the trade turned to recent corpses of criminals or Christians which were dried in the sun and powdered up. 'Mummy' was also a painter's requisite, for pitch from Egyptian tombs was thought to be immune from cracking with age.

By the end of the sixteenth century trade between Egypt and western Europe had grown and diversified and more Europeans were going there and reporting on what they saw. They were sometimes very inaccurate, and even utterly forged accounts were circulated, written by people who had never set foot in Egypt, but as time went by these travellers' tales became a better guide for European scholarship to ancient Egypt than the Bible and the classical authorities. In 1505, twelve years before the Turkish rule, a German knight called Martin Baumgarten went to Alexandria—on his way to see the Holy Sepulchre in Jerusalem. He examined an obelisk, which is now in New York, and made what were perhaps the last sensible remarks on the likely meaning of the hieroglyphs that were to be uttered for two hundred and fifty years. He said that the obelisk was: 'full of figures of living creatures and other things, which plainly shows that the Egyptians of old made use of such instead of letters'.

An Englishman, George Sandys, who saw Baumgarten's obelisk at Alexandria and noted another lying by 'half buried in rubbish'—it now stands on the London Embankment—was the first man to bring back reliable drawings of the pyramids and Sphinx in 1610. John Greaves, professor of astronomy and mathematics at Oxford, examined and drew the Great Pyramid in 1638 with a freshly objective eye. He rejected esoteric explanations for its existence and concluded that it was a royal tomb, built to last.

If Shakespeare had been able to read Greaves' account, he would not have put a window in a pyramid. But the travellers' descriptions brought no progress with the problem of the hieroglyphs. Unfortunately, these were often copied in a slip-shod and inaccurate way—perhaps because few took them seriously as an everyday form of writing and preferred to regard them as arcane symbolism.

For the more adventurous European scholar there was one more source of information about ancient Egypt, to be added to the Bible, the classics and the travellers' tales: this was study of the Coptic language. Coptic was still spoken and even understood until the seventeenth century AD. It is still voiced today, but not understood, in the services of the Coptic Church. It is a direct descendant of the ancient Egyptian language and knowledge of it was to make all the difference to Champollion's successful work. Athanasius Kircher, in the early seventeenth century, knew Coptic, but it did not help him with his fanciful translations of the hieroglyphs.

This German Jesuit's rendering of what we know was simply the hiero-glyphic version of one of the Roman emperor's titles 'Autocrator' (itself a Greek word, related to our 'autocrat') reads thus: 'The originator of all moisture and all vegetation is Osiris, whose creative power was brought to this Kingdom by the holy Mophtha'. Kircher was probably reworking what he knew of Egyptian religion from Plutarch's 'Isis and Osiris', a very hellenized account of the subject.

Against this wholly misguided rendering may be set Robert Huntingdon's suggestion (he was in Egypt between 1670 and 1681) that the hieroglyphs were not abstract symbols of mystical import—in which he was right—but were ideograms, where a single sign always represented an entire word or idea—in which he was wrong.

The secretary of the Society of Antiquaries in London, William Stukeley, was still pessimistic, however, in the 1760s when no progress had been made with the unyielding signs: 'I believe the true knowledge of the hieroglyphics was immersed in the extremist antiquity. . . . The perfect knowledge of them is irrecoverable with the most ancient priests.'

The explorations of merchants and gentleman-scholars were con-tinuing to pay off in a purely archaeological way. New sites were being found and they were sometimes being correctly identified with places mentioned in the Bible and the classics. And a new force had entered on the scene: for the first time agents were being purposely sent out to Egypt to make antiquarian explorations. The French were to the fore in this, in a way foreshadowing Napoleon's venture. In 1672 J. B. Vansleb, a German, visited Egypt in search of antiquities for Louis XIV—he visited the Sakkara bird-mummy galleries which have been re-discovered by later explorers. And the Jesuit Claude Sicard was charged in the early eighteenth century with making a complete investigation of ancient monuments in Egypt, co-incidentally converting to Christianity as he went. He was the first to identify correctly the site of ancient Thebes at Luxor and Karnak.

For the British, that famous explorer who found the source of the Blue Nile, James Bruce, arrived in Egypt in 1768. He visited Thebes and the Valley of the Kings, where Tutankhamun's tomb was to be found a century and a half later, before going up to Aswan and into Nubia. At Thebes he was shrewd enough to note that ancient Egyptian sign-writing came in three forms: what he called 'hieroglyphic', 'mummy character' and 'Ethiopic'. Nowadays these are respectively known as hieroglyphic, hieratic and demotic. The Rosetta Stone carries, above its Greek register, two of them: the 'classical' and formal hieroglyphic and the everyday late-period demotic.

So, by the time of Napoleon's expedition, Egypt was becoming very well known to the European world. Collections of antiquities brought back from Egypt were growing in European countries. When the British

Museum opened in 1762, there were already papyri and statuettes and small objects from Egypt in its collections.

But still, in the early 1800s, anyone writing one of the popular 'universal histories' of the day was scarcely in any better position to reach beyond the much-worn biblical and classical sources employed by the Renaissance writers when it came to matters of real chronologies and accurate dates for the events of Egyptian history or to giving a true picture of the everyday lives and beliefs of the ancient Egyptians. This all waited on the decipherment of the language and on the establishment of a rationalized archaeological study of the remains themselves.

On the eve of Napoleon's expedition to Egypt, the radical Comte de Volney—who had visited Egypt and perhaps seen Egyptian peasants making free of their cultural heritage for casual building operations or burning bits of it for lime—reflected that 'the philosopher cannot help smiling at the secret malice of fate, that gives back to the people what cost them so much misery, and that assigns to the most humble of their needs the pride of useless luxury'. As well as serving as a salutary warning against too much concern to rescue at all costs the memorials of an obsolete culture, de Volney's observation surely reflects the frustration felt by the educated inquirers of his time in the face of the abundant remains of a vanished civilization that simply could not be elucidated. Decipherment of the hieroglyphs was vital to any further understanding of ancient Egypt.

Chapter II The Land of Egypt and the First Egyptians

Since the alteration of climatic conditions that followed upon the end of the last ice age some ten thousand years ago, Egypt has enjoyed an unusual physical situation. As an habitable country, it has existed since then only because of the presence of the river Nile. The Nile in Egypt is an 'exotic' stream, in the sense that the source of its waters lies right outside the boundaries of the country it flows through and serves. Egypt as a whole experiences a very low rainfall. Without the Nile, Egypt would now be, not the 'Black Land' that the ancient Egyptians called it— 'Kemet'—by virtue of its rich and productive mud, but simply a desert. The country is indeed, as Herodotus dubbed it, 'the Gift of the Nile'.

The Nile is the second longest waterway of the world, exceeded only by the Mississippi—Missouri system, and the second longest river as such, with only the Amazon a little longer. Its Egyptian reaches, north from the First Cataract where the Nile tumbles over a rocky bed for a space, approach a thousand kilometres in length before flowing out through the several streams of the Delta into the Mediterranean sea, which the ancient Egyptians graphically called 'the Great Green'. The Nile is fed by the waters of several tributaries and rivers. Leaving lake Victoria, the White Nile flows north, partly through the diffuse swamps of the Sudd, and is then served by two tributaries and the inflow of the river Sobat; later on it flows with the Blue Nile and, after Khartum, the Atbara, to become the single Nile proper without further contributory waters until it reaches the Mediterranean. Since the close of the last ice age, the Blue Nile and the Atbara have accounted for the Nile's annual flood: the summer rains in the Ethiopian highlands swell these two streams until their great volume of water pens up the White Nile's flow in the south and sends up the level of the river throughout the length of Egypt; from September, when the rains cease to supply the Blue Nile and Atbara, the waters of the White Nile resume their flow until the following May, preventing too rapid a drop in the level created by the Blue Nile and Atbara and maintaining the Egyptian river over the winter months.

Before the end of the ice age, this pattern was probably not nearly so clear-cut. Conditions were wetter than today during the 'pluvial' or rainy period which corresponds in Africa with the glaciation of Europe, and there was probably a winter flood due to rains in the Sudan that balanced out the flood created by the summer highland rains of Ethiopia and led to a considerably moister situation all the year round. Although partly obscured by inevitable fluctuations, the tendency has been for Egypt to become progressively drier in climate since the peak of the last ice age—crocodiles still occurred as far north as Palestine in immediately post-glacial times, and people hunted game in the now dry Sinai peninsula. Indeed conditions were wetter in Egypt than they are today well down into historical times: until about 2400 BC, areas which are now quite arid on the margins of the flood-plain still supported groups of hunting or purely pastoral peoples. Acacia and sycamore roots have been found on the low desert fringes of the river beyond the present flood-plain. The tombs of the Old Kingdom at Sakkara, in particular, seem to reveal an Egypt of four thousand years or so ago that was wetter than today—

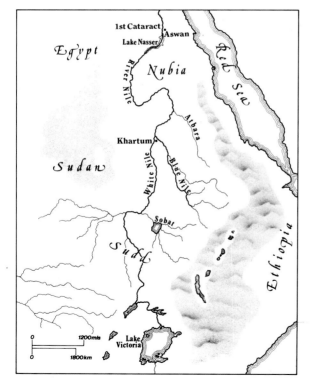

The headwaters of the Nile.

27

with hippopotamus, crocodile, water birds, and lotus and reed swamps. But probably such areas were never all that extensive in historical times, even if they were favourite sporting grounds for the rich.

On the whole, Egyptian geography achieved its present character with the ending of the ice age. The coastline of the Mediterranean has not changed since about 8000 BC when the sea level rose again with the melting of the northern glaciers and the course of the Nile itself has altered by no more than a mile or so since those days, except where the Delta streams have wandered or the river has been artificially modified by the hand of man. The Nile's river bed, however, has been independently rising over the years due to the deposition of silt (though the Aswan High Dam may now largely remove these silts from the water) and this raised water level has threatened some monuments which were originally built well above the water-table: the great Hypostyle Hall at the Karnak temple has suffered badly from damp.

The land of Egypt has three major features: the flood-plain of the river and the Delta; the low desert borders of the river; and the desert uplands beyond these lower margins. During the wetter 'pluvial' periods of the ice age all three zones may well have been occupied by man. The very earliest forms of man-made tools, which have been found in other parts of Africa, are not met with in Egypt, nor are the remains of the earliest forms of man, like the 'Australopithecines' of South and east Africa (though such remains have been discovered further east, showing that Egypt may possibly have been within the range of our earliest ancestors). From the Fayum region—what is left, about 100 kilometres to the south-west of Cairo, of a once extensive lake in wetter days—have come the remains of the world's earliest known ape, around thirty million years old; and from the same place and of about the same age, come the remains of *Propliopithecus* which may just possibly be a candidate for the remote ancestry of the human line. Of the bones of all the early forms of man—from the Australopithecines through the *erectus* stage ('Peking Man' type) to the Neanderthal form of *Homo sapiens*—there is no trace at all in Egypt.

But there is plenty of evidence for prehistoric human activity all over Egypt: the stone tools, if not the bones, of early man have survived there. The earliest stages are widespread, they are not confined like the remains of later human occupation to the immediate vicinity of the river. From the Kharga Oasis, south of the Fayum and west of Luxor, come handaxes of a simple type which also occur in a stranded shore-line of the Nile 30 metres above its present level, formed at a time when a greater river flowed into a higher sea. In the lower ancient shore-lines there occur progressively finer handaxes and better made flakes of flint which eventually take over from the axes as the predominant type of tool. From geologically later deposits of the river and from the lower shore-lines of the Fayum

Old Kingdom tombs like Ti's depict an Egypt in whose marshes swamp life,
including even the hippopotamus, still richly flourished in the third millennium BC.
Hunting in the marshes was a favourite sport of kings and nobles.

Above *Prehistoric rock pictures from parts of Egypt reveal a wetter and lusher climate in the past, with the presence of giraffe and other wild-life that never occurred in Egypt in historical times, perhaps as a result of over-hunting.*

Left *A pot from the later prehistoric period of Egypt shows that boats were plying on the Nile and, no doubt, drawing together the communities along the river at an early date.*

lake come little flint tools of a fine geometric type which seem to have developed out of the earlier flakes. These late forms belong to the last few thousand years of the ice age, about ten thousand years ago, and many important discoveries of this microlithic geometric material have been made in recent years as a result of the international archaeological efforts undertaken in Nubia before the water of lake Nasser rose behind the new Aswan High Dam. Whereas the handaxes, belonging to what is known as the 'Lower Palaeolithic' period, and the big flakes of the 'Middle Palaeolithic', are found away from the river and even up on the desert plateau, the later 'Upper Palaeolithic' pieces are concentrated on the Nile flood-plain and show that, by late ice age times, the climate was on the whole tending towards drier conditions than before, in which the oases and wadis (seasonal water courses) of wetter times were becoming less and less habitable. Despite the lack of any human remains from this period, we may assume that the makers of the late Upper Palaeolithic tools were *Homo sapiens* of modern form like the present peoples of the world. It is probable that the makers of the Middle Palaeolithic material were, in part, of the earlier, Neanderthal sort of *Homo sapiens*, while the Lower Palaeolithic toolmakers were possibly the older *Homo erectus* forms like the 'Peking Men' of China.

Though the Upper Palaeolithic people of the end of the ice age seem to have lived nearer to the Nile than their ancestors had done, hunting the rich fauna that lived along the river banks or came down to drink (it included elephant and giraffe before things became too dessicated), they would not have been nearly so completely tied to the river as their agricultural successors were to be. For the farmers, everything depended upon being on the spot when the Nile deposited its annual load of fertilizing mud. Farming and the domestication of animals probably did not begin in Egypt itself, but were introduced there after the pattern of prior developments elsewhere. It is generally accepted that the area known as 'The Fertile Crescent', a two-horned region lying across the headwaters of the Tigris and Euphrates from the Zagros Mountains in the east to the south-east corner of Anatolia and the Mediterranean coast in the west, is the most likely site of the development of agriculture in the eastern Mediterranean region. (Of course, the Far Eastern and American developments of agriculture and pastoralism were almost certainly independent of the eastern Mediterranean one: the causes of the so-called 'Neolithic Revolutions' which occurred around the world in the climatically favourable period following the end of the ice age are imperfectly understood, but are probably dependent upon the emergence of modern *Homo sapiens*, with his progressively sophisticated technological and intellectual and inventive traits, who could exploit the opportunity offered by nature better than his ancestors). The Fertile Crescent is a prime candidate for the area in which the cultivation of plants began because in it there uniquely overlap the natural distribution regions of the wild prototypes of wheat and barley which appear to have been the first domesticated plants and were often grown together by the first farmers. And this same area of the Near East is co-incidentally the one in which the wild ancestors of the first domesticated animals like sheep and goat lived. Egypt had no wild sheep or goat forms ancestral to the domesticated species, nor did the wild prototypes of wheat and barley occur.

None the less, the Nile Valley was a first-rate location for the development of an agriculturally-based economy. Of course, the hunters of earlier times did not disappear overnight when farming became established—indeed bands of hunting peoples persisted right down into historical times in Egypt and thrived as long as the desert wadis on the fringe of the farmlands and the Delta creeks made the hunter-gatherer life possible. To the ancient Egyptians of the settled and civilized valley these latter-day hunters seemed a rough and ready lot and they were inclined to poke fun at them: a statue shows a pair of them festooned with fish and fowl and uncouthly bearded. But the progressive dessication of the desert margins reduced the scope of the hunters' life and the clear economic superiority of farming in terms of surplus wealth soon turned the communities of post-glacial Egypt into farmers for the most part.

It is no longer possible to observe how perfectly was the Nile's seasonal behaviour attuned to the interests of the first farmers. In the last century, the resourceful and ambitious Mohamed Ali drastically altered the Nile's seasonal pattern when—in the interest of his cotton-growing enterprises—he plumped henceforth for perennial as opposed to seasonal irrigation of the countryside. Instead of allowing the single summer flood, peaking in August, to water the fields (and fill up basins for the rest of the year), he initiated a programme of barrage-building—first of all in the Delta, later on up river at Asyut and Aswan—in order to save back the waters of the annual flood and then to distribute them evenly throughout the year. This programme has reached its present peak of achievement in the new Aswan High Dam and in lake Nasser which lies behind it. The lake is, additionally, full of fish and the dam generates power for all Egypt as well as controlling the river, although its silt-filtering action, robbing the Nile of some of its fertile load, will need attention.

Before these man-made alterations to the river's yearly career were carried out, the level of the waters rose each August along the Nile's banks, from Aswan down to the Delta, by an average of about six metres from lowest to highest levels. The ancient Egyptians were so keen to plot the course of the all-important flood that they installed a so-called 'Nilometer' at Aswan to record and predict levels. The present one dates from the latter days of ancient Egypt, but the site was in use in earlier times. When the waters came up, they rapidly overflowed the banks of the winter river and flooded out over the whole Nile plain. As soon as the

32

The rich dark soil of the Nile Valley, as black today as when it gave to Egypt one of its ancient names 'The Black Land', still provides the agricultural basis of Egyptian life.

The Step Pyramid complex of Djoser includes much more than the pyramid itself:
around the world's first major stone building are ranged stone-built 'dummy'
replicas of storehouses and chapels in which wooden prototypes have been realized
in the new and more difficult material; the whole was surrounded by a high
perimeter wall with one entrance.

water was widely spread over the flood-plain, the river lost much of its energy and matter-carrying capacity. The result was that the main deposition of material carried in the river occurred along the banks of the winter stream, forming ridges of land that marked the main course of the Nile. These ridges stood up above the surrounding flood-plain and, of course, they were the first bits of dry land to emerge from the river as the inundation subsided in September. This fact impressed itself deeply on the ancient Egyptian consciousness as an image not merely of the annual restoration of their land but, more fundamentally, as the mythological picture of what had occurred at the very creation of the world itself, rising out of the waters of chaos. In the Delta a similar situation to this ridging of the river banks occurred when the water spread out via many streams and creeks, creating swamps that were perennially wet but separated by bars of deposits.

The ridges along the banks of the Upper Egyptian Nile and the bars of the Delta were ideally suited to agricultural settlement; at the most they were only very briefly submerged during the flood and they were terrifically fertile, carrying woods of Nile acacia and willow and sycamore. The low desert margins of the river were almost equally attractive. Men could live on both areas and sow their seeds simply by throwing them into the mud left by the receding waters of the inundation. In a season, before the waters rose again, the crop would grow tall and be harvested. This was the yearly round of the Nile-side farmers and, if the re-emergence of the ridges of land from the waters of the flood generated the mythological image of the creation and recreation of the world, then similarly the assured yearly growth of the sown seed and yearly cutting down of the crop in harvest gave to the ancient Egyptian imagination the idea of the resurrection-cycle of the corn-god Osiris who plays so large a part in Egyptian religion, and who has left something of himself behind in the mythological reworkings of later cultures. A shallow wooden tray in the characteristic form of Osiris was filled with Nile mud and scattered with seeds to sprout in unseen resurrection in the tomb of Tutankhamun.

The Nile was so ready-made and dependable an agricultural agent that its occasional failures were impressive and alarming. There are records of years of low Nile from late Old Kingdom times, in about 2300 BC when the last stage of post-glacial dessication was being achieved. Low Niles brought starvation and may have contributed to the crisis in which the Old Kingdom collapsed. Joseph's 'lean years' of the Bible probably reflect an incidence of low Niles.

Farming, in both its agricultural and pastoral aspects, grew up in the first place among people not unlike the late Upper Palaeolithic microlith-makers of Upper Egypt about ten thousand years ago. Peoples of this sort were spread out all over Europe and the Near and Middle East. They were fully modern *Homo sapiens* types, whose general ancestors

The ancient Egyptians never lost sight of the vital importance of agriculture and the yearly renewal of their crops: in the tomb of Tutankhamun a shallow tray in the form of the resurrection-god Osiris, identified with the Nile and its fertility, has sprouted vegetation from its filling of Nile mud in an image of the restoration of life and abundance.

had included the painters of the French caves like Lascaux, where art and magic and perhaps religion make their first appearance in the world. The gradual change in the economy of these peoples from hunting and gathering towards pastoralism and agriculture, domesticating animals and cultivating plants, can be charted at various places in the area of the Fertile Crescent. Around 9000 BC, at Zawi Chemi-Shanidar in northern Iraq, people equipped with this general microlithic flint tool-kit appear in the archaeological record sporting in addition querns and mortars clearly intended for the preparation of grain, whether collected wild or truly cultivated. The remains of their occupation also indicate that they had domesticated the sheep by this time: the first domesticated animal (excluding perhaps the dog) of human history. At about the same date of 9000 BC, in the foothills of the Zagros mountains at Karim Shahir, both dogs and sheep seem to have been domesticated and wheat and barley were perhaps being cultivated as opposed to simply being gathered in quantity. Further south towards the Persian Gulf, over the next thousand years or so, the progress of agriculture and of the domestication of goats and sheep can be charted at such sites as Ali Kosh and Ganj Dareh.

Between Zawi Chemi-Shanidar and these southerly sites, farming innovations are even clearer at the site of Jarmo: before long, there were permanent settlements of mud huts here with domesticated goats, sheep and pigs, while the proper cultivation of crops was under way. It is likely that in this area agriculture did lag a little behind pastoralism in initial development, but the opposite may have been true at the other end of the Fertile Crescent. Certainly in Palestine, but with extensions perhaps into southern Anatolia and definitely into Sinai, the people named after Wadi-en-Natuf, the Natufians, were taking the first steps on the way to the agricultural economy around 9000 BC. They are important because they supply the background developments to the whole progress of the 'Neolithic' farming way of life in the Mediterranean region. These hunters lived both in caves and on open sites and once again, alongside their microlith-tipped hunting kit, they additionally possessed some tools suggestive of at least an intensive plant-gathering economy: there are pestles and mortars, bone handles into which reaping-knife blades could be set and many little blades of flint with the characteristic lustre on their edges that comes from reaping cereal stalks. They were probably not cultivating these cereals, however, and they possessed no domestic animals. Nevertheless, the size of some of their cemeteries suggests considerable semi-permanent or permanent settlements, as does the paving and walling with which they furnished one of their sites. Some time after 9000 BC a Natufian group had an encampment around the spring that once lay at the base of what later became the great heaped 'tell' of Jericho. The Natufian remains are overlain by those of some definite farmers whose flints show them to have almost certainly been descended from the Natufian hunters. By 7000 BC, as determined by the carbon-14 method of dating organic remains, the existence of agriculture as such is clearly demonstrated in Jordan and Anatolia and Iran by the presence of the carbonized remains of domesticated plants. A thousand years later, considerable and sophisticated settlements, real townships with shrines and sometimes fortifications, existed in all these areas where early agricultural settlements had preceded them. In the sixth millennium BC, the earliest farmers of Cyprus and mainland Greece appear, initiating the course of the 'Neolithic Revolution' in the rest of Europe. Pottery, which had been absent in the earliest farming communities, and the early stages of metal-working, became established at this time.

In Egypt, the Neolithic period proper—the time when clearly defined farming was in operation in the Nile Valley and the Delta—began around 5000 BC. In the three thousand years that separate the earliest Neolithic from the late Upper Palaeolithic of the end of the ice age, the country had no doubt gone on being inhabited, but evidence from this 'Mesolithic' period is rather scanty. There are some Mesolithic traces well down south around the Second Cataract of the Nile and at sites near Cairo and there must be more evidence yet to come to light. The situation must have been much as it was at the same time in Europe and among the very earliest Zagros Mountain groups and the Natufians: a sort of 'pre-Neolithic', in which the groundwork for crop-cultivation and domestication of animals was being achieved. The Mesolithic hunters of the Cairo area were equipped in a way that resembles the Natufians.

Some of the grain-crops cultivated in Egypt in the Neolithic period were not based on native prototypes and, among the domesticated animals, the sheep was an Asiatic introduction too. It is not necessary, however, to imagine any invasion or diffusion of better endowed peoples into Egypt from western Asia to explain the development of the Egyptian farming economy. It is probably rather a case of a sharing of ideas across the ancient world among peoples whose own developments made them ready to participate in the innovations of the time. People are everywhere and at all times inventive and resourceful unless there is some powerful reason or excuse not to be: in the case of the spread of farming, the 'pre-Neolithic' background pattern was widely established after the end of the ice age and adoption of the new way of life could take place very rapidly.

In Egypt, the shrinking of the habitable land with the dessication of post-glacial times must have wrought a considerable social mix among the human groups associated with the Nile, and have given incentive to the search for increasingly productive ways of living along the river. Earlier in this century it was popular, after the anthropological fashion of the day, to try to identify the 'racial' strands that had gone to make up the ancient Egyptian population; this is probably not a very worthwhile pursuit, beyond noticing that a southerly 'African' type mixes in Egypt

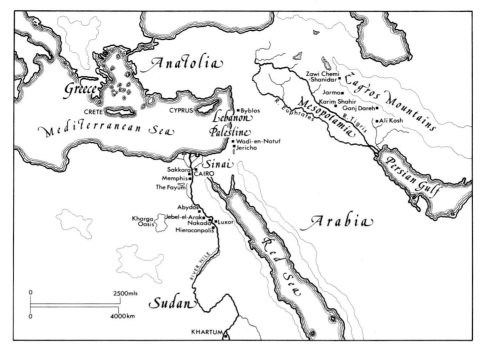

The 'Fertile Crescent' and the sites of early farming and settled life.

with a northerly 'Mediterranean' one. Linguistically, it is possible to place the ancient Egyptian language in the 'Afro-Asian' family, to which also belong the extensive Berber tongues of north and west Africa, the Cushitic and Chadic languages to the south of Egypt and the Semitic group (to which Hebrew and Arabic belong). Though sharing most grammatical features in common with the Semitic group, in particular, ancient Egyptian differs in vocabulary and other features in an irregular enough way to suggest a long separation from the rest of its family—so probably the Nile Valley, while never being out of touch with the cultures of the surrounding lands, has long enjoyed a substantial individuality of its own.

The peculiar geography of Egypt and the distinctive manner in which the Nile supports life there made from the first for some characteristically Egyptian developments in life-style. Although Egypt did not become a centralized monarchy under a single king (later called 'pharaoh' which means 'great house' rather in the way that the Ottoman Empire was alluded to as 'the Porte') until the unification of the country at the very beginning of historical times, there was probably a tradition of powerful chieftainship from the earliest Neolithic times. It is tempting to see in such an institution an essentially *African* trait in the development of

39

ancient Egypt—the pharaohs of history were not just kings like their counterparts in the other early civilizations of the ancient world; they were divine rulers, the sons and incarnations of the deity. This is an aspect they share with the rain-maker, magic-working kings of the rest of Africa, whose role is to guarantee the well-being of their people by the exercise of divine powers. A considerable degree of social organization was required as soon as serious farming was adopted to carry out the necessary work of levelling the fields after the flood, holding back reserves of water, opening up irrigation channels, sowing and reaping the crop. Man-made modifications of the Nile Valley have their origins in the Egyptian Neolithic. It is possible that the earlier phases of the 'Neolithic Revolution' were carried out in some parts of the world in an egalitarian and 'democratic' fashion that perpetuated for a time the social habits of the hunters who fathered the first farmers. Class divisions made their appearance almost everywhere once surpluses of wealth made it possible— and, in the interests of increasing wealth, necessary—for groups of priests and nobles to direct and exploit the labours of the rest of the community. In Egypt, it seems likely that the groups of nobles and priests were from the first presided over by the sort of divine chieftains who created the later pharaonic tradition, decked in an ideology of kingship and divinity that ramified through the whole of ancient Egyptian life. In prehistoric days, there were probably many such kings ruling over many little communities along the Nile: all the diverse religious traditions of historical times bear witness to the previous cultural fragmentation of the country. The first king of a single, united Egypt is traditionally called Menes (from the history written by Manetho in the Greek Period) and it is significant to see him credited with the first damming of the Nile. In this tradition the peculiar influence of the river upon the civilization it supported is high-lighted at the very beginning of Egyptian history. Perhaps even those colossal monuments of the first phase of Egyptian history, the pyramids at Giza, which were built within five hundred years of Menes' unification, reveal something more of the river's impact upon the Egyptian culture. The Nile may have called forth considerable social organization in order to exploit its agricultural potential, but it did not require attention all the year round—from harvest time to re-inundation life was much less demanding and it has been suggested that the social organization neces-sitated by the winter-to-spring period of intensive work in the fields practically cried out for something to do for the rest of the year. The pyramids may have been an answer to the 'problem' posed by the existence of a socially conscientious work-force with time on its hands: if in winter the community worked under the king's rule for its material survival, then it may have carried on in summer with an ideological expression of this same purpose in the form of the king's eternal symbolic domination over the valley via his pyramid.

The prehistory of ancient Egypt is essentially the story of the coalescence of separate communities along the Nile and in the Delta, first into two separate kingdoms of Upper and Lower Egypt and then into the single state whose first ruler—the traditional Menes—marks the beginning of historical times.

The earliest Neolithic phases are disclosed in Middle and Lower Egypt on the banks of the Fayum lake-depression and in the western region of the Delta; there is a Neolithic site at the inverted tip of the Delta near Cairo; in Upper Egypt, the early Neolithic is featured at sites near Luxor and then further south and finally way down around Khartum. The sites in Lower Egypt appear to be the earlier ones. From these sites come agricultural indicators like flint sickles, clay-lined basket silos and evidence of wheat and barley cultivation. The presence of flax suggests that spinning may have been in development. There were domesticated cattle, sheep and goats, pigs and dogs. Leatherwork and weaving were being practised and rather crude pottery was manufactured. These early Egyptian farmers lived in oval mud huts organized into villages and they buried their dead inside these villages. It seems that the dead were sometimes supplied with some cereal-grains, in a way that points up the agricultural pre-occupations of these people and perhaps foreshadows the Osiris resurrection-cult already mentioned in connection with Tutankhamun's sprouting Osiriform tray. Radiocarbon dating suggests something like 4500 BC for these sites, but it is probable that only traces of the later ones have survived while the earlier sites have gone irrevocably under the Delta silt.

The Neolithic sites near Cairo and in Upper Egypt are probably a few centuries later than those in Lower Egypt. The people living near modern Cairo possessed considerable stoneworking skills, making very fine laurel-leaf flint spearheads and carving stone vessels and 'palettes' (the flat dishes that were used to prepare cosmetics, in particular for eye adornment). In Upper Egypt, the farmers were now burying their dead not within their villages, as the somewhat earlier people of Lower Egypt had done, but in regular necropolises on the desert's edge, mortuary counterparts of the communities of the living. Agricultural land was at a premium in Upper Egypt and these people could not afford to waste plots on their dead. Bodies were buried crouched in an oval pit with a mat covering and sometimes supplied with pots and weapons. Among these pots were some very fine products, in particular the black-topped red ware (seen in the photograph of a crouched burial) that was to go on through the prehistoric period. Nile mud turns red when baked and the black tops are due to inverted firing in ashes. The drying desert sand led to a sort of natural mummification in some of these graves which may have helped to suggest to the people of prehistoric Egypt the notion of preserving the bodies of the dead.

The Predynastic Period, which follows on from the Neolithic with the same contemporaneous north-south distinctions, was the time from about 3800 BC to 3200 BC when the foundations of the historical or dynastic Egyptian civilization were clearly being laid down. This is the period among whose remains many of the traits of the familiar later culture can first be positively identified.

The Fayum Depression is the site of a Lower Egyptian manifestation of the Predynastic: the material here includes beautiful bowls and vases carved from stone in the manner of the Neolithic people from the Cairo area; for the first time there are occasional items of copper; the pots are very varied in form but not particularly well made. In Upper Egypt, the ceramic skills were better developed, but fewer forms of pots were made. The first stage of the Predynastic Period in Upper Egypt coincided with the Fayum Predynastic, but went on to develop without a break into a second phase for which there is no contemporary parallel in Lower Egypt. From the first, the predynastic people of Upper Egypt lived in well-made oval mud huts, which were even equipped with beds. Their graves, moreover, contained a sort of prototype wooden coffin. Among the material goods of these people there now featured occasional metal tools alongside the predominantly flint ones: these metal tools were simply of cold-wrought copper, which could not have been of Nile Valley origin and must have been traded in from the Sudan or from Sinai. Wood was being similarly imported from the Lebanon, where Byblos was perhaps the first site of the development of coastal sea-going boats in the Mediterranean; wood was always scarce in Egypt. The black-topped red pots were now joined by a plain but polished red form, and a technological innovation had been made that was to last throughout Egyptian history—the production of so-called 'Egyptian faïence' which creates a vitrified enamel glaze. Glazed beads also occur: the first incidence of what are really objects of glass. There are more of those cosmetic palettes in the Upper Egyptian Predynastic, together with clay or ivory statuettes of women and carved ivory combs with animal decorations.

The principal sites of the later phase which developed out of the early Upper Egyptian Predynastic are in the region of Abydos. The developed predynastic culture of this area adds a new form of pot to the previously existing black-topped reds and polished reds: a fine red form with white-line decorations sometimes in the form of abstract patterning and sometimes of more naturalistic designs. White on black pots also occur. The naturalistic art includes certain hunting scenes, in particular the hunting of hippopotamuses, that continue in spirit into the Old Kingdom reliefs, and then into the New Kingdom tomb paintings. The eye make-up palettes continued to be carved, anticipating the elaborate specimens which are so important for the interpretation of the beginnings of dynastic history. Very fine flint knives went on being manufactured in this period and some of the graves contain the sort of beautifully carved stone vessels associated with the Lower Egyptian sites, indicating that contact was being well maintained with the northern communities whose archaeological relics of this period we otherwise lack. As yet no writing was being employed in these predynastic societies (at least none was being done in however so rudimentary a form on any pots or palettes that have survived) but there is evidence to suggest that some of the foundations of the hieroglyphic system were being laid. These people possessed a form of mace-head (whether as weapon or piece of regalia) that went completely out of use later on in the Predynastic Period but whose form is retained as a phonetic sign among the hieroglyphs of historical times. It is as though some unrecorded symbol-system that prefigured writing as such had adopted the mace-sign while such maces were still in use and preserved that sign until true writing of a kind that has survived came into being. This piece of evidence suggests that, with regard to writing as with regard to farming, a background of fundamental achievements was being built up throughout the ancient world that would permit of the rapid spread of important new developments as they came along. The Sumerians of Lower Meso-potamia may have developed writing a little earlier than the Egyptians, or the Proto-Elamites further east may have pipped the Sumerians to the post, but there is no need to imagine any importation, lock-stock-and-barrel, of the idea of writing into an Egypt (or anywhere else) that lacked all previous notion of this new invention. As with farming, it is more profitable to recognize a continuum of ideas and skills developing *more or less* simultaneously over a wide but essentially similarly cultured area.

The succeeding stages of the Predynastic Period see the ever in-creasing development of the typically Egyptian culture. The distinction between Upper and Lower Egypt persists, but a common culture shared by both areas gradually emerges. The seat of power seems to shift first north and then south before final unification is achieved.

From the Fayum and from Memphis, near Cairo, comes evidence of a culture destined to spread south and mingle, though perhaps from a position of strength, with the culture just described from the Abydos area, and so to unite into a single ancient Egyptian late predynastic culture. With its earliest appearance, the tombs become characteristically squarer and have more chambers than before. This almost certainly reflects a development in the houses of the living towards more sophisticated forms. The very fine stone vessels of earlier periods are maintained, and precious stones and gold become more frequent. Light-coloured pots with decoration in dark red carry only naturalistic designs, including animals and boats. Interestingly, the boats seem to carry standards, rather like flag poles, topped with animal figures in a way that may prefigure the emblems that distinguished the official regions or 'nomes' of historical Egypt. There is another form of mace-head that features, like the earlier

Below left *On the base of a statue of king Djoser, the ruler's feet trample both the bows that represent the foreign enemies of Egypt and the lapwings that may be the Egyptian people.*

Below right *From the tomb of Tutankhamun, two small statues of the pharaoh portray him in the traditional coned 'white crown' of Upper Egypt and the 'red crown' of the Lower Kingdom.*

Below *The hot dry sands of Egypt can desiccate a body buried in them and so preserve it, like this pre-historic Egyptian, for more than five thousand years.*

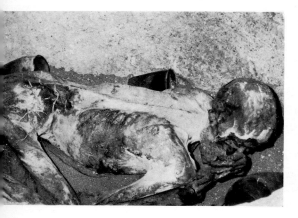

44

one from Abydos, in the historical hieroglyphics. Cosmetic palettes continue, and there is now more use made of metal: the copper chisels needed to carve in stone are found among these people's remains. The first positive signs of the development of Egyptian religions as we later know it come from this Lower Egyptian middle predynastic phase: stone statuary of a falcon god suggests the Horus of history, significantly associated with the sky-god and with the living king, and cow-horned Hathor of love and fertility is hinted at in cow carvings.

This culture seems to have sent its influence south to intermingle with the Upper Egyptian predynastic tradition, in a slow process whereby the pottery forms and mace-head patterns of southern Egypt were gradually replaced by the northern ones. The culture of Egypt as a whole was refining and advancing technologically during this time, around 3400 BC, and although there may have been two provinces, two kingdoms even, in north and south, there gradually emerged a single culture. At first, as we have noted, the 'conquest', if such it may be called, seems to have gone south from Lower Egypt to Upper Egypt. Later on, just before the commencement of historical times, things seem to have gone the other way. At all events, Egypt seems to have long enough remained two distinct countries to have led to its being dubbed by the historical Egyptians: 'the Two Lands'. Kings and pharaohs went on wearing a double crown to symbolize the union of these two lands: a combination ᵇ of the Upper ◢ 'white' and Lower ⩛ 'red' crowns of the predynastic kingdoms that went on figuring separately in later times. Tutankhamun's images from his tomb made fifteen hundred years after the unification show him in both crowns. The historical crowns carried, moreover, the images of the goddesses both of Upper and Lower Egypt—the Vulture and the Cobra. In times of trouble, Egypt was always likely to return to the division that marked its earlier days.

The Nile waterway must have been a powerful impetus towards unification. It seems that the historians of the Old Kingdom knew perfectly well who the separate kings of Upper and Lower Egypt were before the unification took place. We would know them too, but the annals of the Old Kingdom have only survived in fragmentary form. The biggest piece of one of these Old Kingdom king-lists is now in Palermo and called the Palermo Stone. The damage leaves us with the names of just seven kings of Lower Egypt and five of Upper. We do not know whether the Old Kingdom writers were benefiting from an oral tradition when they compiled their lists or whether some ancient written tradition unknown to us was their basis.

Writing does seem to have been in use in Sumer at least, in an imperishable medium, before it was employed in Egypt. The earliest use of hieroglyphs in Egypt co-incides with or immediately pre-dates the unification, in about 3100 BC. Since before 5000 BC there had been villages and townships of mud-brick on the Tigris-Euphrates plain. The Sumerians may well have developed their distinctive culture 'in situ' in Mesopotamia and by 3000 BC they probably had kings—if not on the divine scale Egypt was to know—and certainly a well-developed form of writing. The earliest Sumerian pictographs (a primitive stage of writing simply showing what is intended) date from perhaps 3500 BC. It has been claimed that this purely pictogram phase is missing from Egyptian hieroglyphs, which also carry a strong phonetic element from the start, and that the Egyptians may have derived some fairly elaborated ideas from the Sumerians. A Mesopotamian cylinder seal has been found in a predynastic Egyptian grave and it is certainly true that some immediately predynastic or early dynastic objects from Egypt, like the Jebel el-Arak knife handle (if we can rely upon its evidence) with its Sumerian-style hero killing lions, do seem to reflect a Mesopotamian influence on style. It is equally true to say that from the first there are many purely Egyptian stylistic traits on these same objects, and it is worth remembering that whatever the influences of Sumer upon Egypt may have been, the Egyptians possessed a quite distinctive culture of their own. Sumer, for instance, never enjoyed the rule of a single god-king like Egypt's in place of its priests and war-leader kings.

The best that we can do to trace the apparent victory of the Upper Egyptian Kingdom over the Lower one is to review a collection of mace-heads and palettes, all from Hieraconpolis in Upper Egypt. All these objects come from the archaeological levels of the first temple of Horus on this site. One pear-shaped mace-head shows a figure, presumably a king, wearing what later came to be known as the 'white crown' of Upper Egypt ◢ and seemingly engaged on some piece of ritual connected with

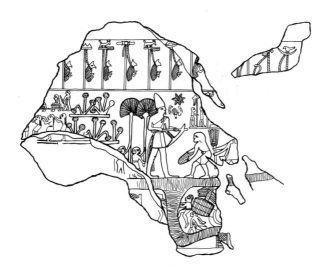

The mace head of the Scorpion King.

Above and next page *The two faces
of the Narmer Palette, from the very
earliest days of Egyptian history, picture
a conqueror who wears both the conicle
'white crown' of the South (above) and the
elaborate 'red crown' of the northerly
region (next page). Narmer may have been the
king who finally united the 'Two Lands'.*

Left *The mace-head of the Scorpion
King probably pre-dates the unification
of Egypt.*

47

One side of the Narmer Palette shows a conquerer wearing the 'red crown' of the North.

48

an agricultural festival or annual event, perhaps the cutting of the first sod of earth for an irrigation channel. Slightly above and just to the right of his face is a hieroglyph, in the form of a scorpion. We do not know how this was meant to be interpreted and we cannot give this king a properly pronounced name: he is simply the Scorpion King. Above him hang bows and lapwings, in a way suggesting that he has conquered them—on later monuments, like the statue base of king Djoser of the Step Pyramid, bows came to signify foreigners and lapwings some part at least of the Egyptian population. So presumably the Scorpion King is laying claim to have conquered some foreign enemy and some Egyptians too, meaning most likely the northerners of Lower Egypt. Also from Hieraconpolis, the famous Narmer Palette shows—this time to the accompaniment of some of the earliest readable hieroglyphs—king Nar-mer (or Meri-nar—his hieroglyphs are again just in front of his face) on the one side wearing the white crown of Upper Egypt and striking his enemies dead and on the other side inspecting some decapitated corpses as he wears the red crown of Lower Egypt. These enemies may well represent the Lower Egyptians themselves, though the palette also makes clear that he has vanquished some foreign enemies too, represented by the fortresses assailed by the bull at the bottom of the side with the white-crowned figure. It is tempting to see in the Scorpion mace-head the beginnings of the South's northern conquest and in the Narmer Palette the full achievement of that victory—this interpretation would make Narmer the traditional 'Menes' of the Greek Period historian. As it happens, yet another mace-head from Hieraconpolis shows the Scorpion King too in the red crown of Lower Egypt and so makes a simple identification impossible. Perhaps a certain amount of ebb and flow occurred in the relations of the two kingdoms before unification and Menes is a conflation representing the accomplishments of several kings: at all events, Egypt became a fully unified kingdom under a single divine ruler around 3100 BC and was already by this time manifesting in a mature form that distinctive culture that was to persist essentially for three thousand years.

This civilization was a literate one with an advanced system of writing that makes it a fully historical entity open to the usual sort of investigation that historians can bring to bear upon the record of the past. For all that, ancient Egypt was fated to remain an almost complete mystery until the last century of our own era.

Chapter III   Champollion's Decipherment and the Beginnings of Archaeology

The importance of the Rosetta Stone for the understanding of ancient Egypt was recognized as soon as it was found and scholars all over Europe were falling over themselves to get to work on copies of it. There was a widespread conviction that this bi-lingual text would be, as the 'Courier d'Egypte' had put it, 'the key' to the ancient language. The Greek portion of it itself proclaimed that this decree was to be posted up in Egyptian and Greek throughout the country: another such stone with the same texts was indeed found at Nubayrah in Lower Egypt later in the last century.

There is still today a general tendency to regard the Rosetta Stone as itself an automatic key to the ancient Egyptian language. It is not as simple as that. Unfamiliar languages have been translated before now without bi-lingual keys—the Linear B of Crete was cracked by purely internal means on the assumption that it was some sort of Greek. And the story of the progress made by various scholars on the inscriptions of the Rosetta Stone demonstrates that something more than simply having the three versions of the same message was needed to unlock the secrets of the ancient Egyptian tongue.

Working 'in the field' at Thebes in the 1760s, James Bruce had proposed a three-fold classification for the writing-systems of ancient Egypt: what we now call hieroglyphic, hieratic and demotic. In England, Bishop William Warburton had already suggested that the more 'long-hand' hieratic was really an easier way of writing the time-consuming and complicated hieroglyphs. He was correct in this view, as he was also right in regarding the hieroglyphs as a practical method of writing and not as priestly mumbo-jumbo. The Rosetta Stone does not carry any hieratic, but rather a demotic version of the text in addition to the hiero-glyphic one. This very cursive demotic script (even specialists find it troublesome to read today) evolved out of the hieratic 'long-hand' in

King Cheops is known today
in only one surviving
representation: a small ivory
statuette in the Cairo
Museum which hardly
qualifies as a likeness of the
mighty ruler who caused the
Great Pyramid to be con-
structed. The statuette does
not come from his pyramid
or indeed from Giza at all,
but from Abydos.

Next page *The Grand Gallery
of the Great Pyramid is a
unique feature in architectural
concept among the Egyptian
pyramids. 45 metres long
and 8·5 high, ascending at
an angle of 26°, it may have
served as a storage space for
the blocks that were to plug
the entrance corridor leading
into the interior of the
pyramid. At the top of the
Grand Gallery, a passage
leads into the sombre black-
granite burial chamber.*

about 700 BC. The hieratic seems to be about as old as the hieroglyphs themselves, both going back to about 3100 BC (hieroglyphs were last carved at Philae in the fourth century AD).

The demotic section in the middle of the Rosetta Stone is the best preserved text: the Greek at the bottom is partly damaged; but there is only about a third of the original hieroglyphic text at the top. The early workers accordingly plumped for attempts to make sense of the demotic. This accidental steering of effort towards the demotic looks unfortunate in retrospect because we now know how difficult the demotic is to handle. The first man to make some headway with it was the French orientalist, Sylvestre de Sacy. By 1802, de Sacy had succeeded in identifying the demotic sign-groups spelling Ptolemy, Alexander and Alexandria, but he could not isolate within these groups the individual signs that correspond with the Greek ones.

Again, in 1802, the Swedish diplomat Johnann David Åkerblad had achieved the demotic correspondences for the Greek names Arsinoë, Berenike and Aëtos. He went further than de Sacy in actually getting out a demotic alphabet of 29 letters, of which about half are correctly identified. He mistakenly thought demotic to be entirely alphabetic (that is, one sign equals one letter as in our language), but at least he had demonstrated that it is partially so. He didn't know that demotic is distantly derived from hieroglyphic and he went to the other extreme with the hieroglyphs in regarding them as entirely pictographic (that is, simply representing the things they show) and, beyond that, symbolic in a holy fashion. Significantly, however, he did get out the demotic renderings of 'temple', 'love', 'Greek' and 'Egyptian' and related these words to their known Coptic equivalents. He was using his knowledge of Coptic (the last descendant of the ancient Egyptian tongue, and about as like it as modern English is like Anglo-Saxon) to check his identification of demotic words with Greek ones upon the Rosetta Stone. Champollion was to extend this principle with devastating effectiveness.

An Englishman has a good claim to have taken the first decisive steps on the road to understanding the hieroglyphs—so good is his claim that he has been put up to challenge Champollion's role by some writers. He was Thomas Young, a brilliant linguist and polymath, famous for originating the wave-theory of light. He too knew Coptic and he too first turned to the demotic section of the Rosetta Stone. He started work in 1814 and by the time he wrote an article for the 1819 Encyclopaedia Britannica on the subject, he had covered a lot of ground. He did not rely entirely on the Rosetta Stone—in 1816 he made the acquaintance of an English country-gentleman who had already copied the inscriptions on an obelisk which he eventually brought back from Egypt and set up on his Dorsetshire estate at Kingston Lacey. It was an obelisk from Philae which carried Greek and hieroglyphic inscriptions. Young still believed that the hiero-

53

Above *Thomas Young was the talented English 'jack of all trades' who first glimpsed the principles of the hieroglyphic system.*

Above *At Kingston Lacey in Dorset still stands the obelisk from Philae which guided Young and Champollion towards the decipherment of the hieroglyphs.*

Right *Champollion, the brilliant and single-minded French linguist, finally deciphered the ancient Egyptian hieroglyphs in the 1820s.*

glyphic form was really a matter of pictograms and symbolism but he took an important step forward in modifying this view to include the possibility that the ancient Egyptians might have been prepared to use hieroglyphs in a purely phonetic way for just one purpose: to render names of foreign origin. A Dane had already suggested that the names of the Ptolemaic rulers mentioned in the Greek part of the inscriptions on the Rosetta Stone, (the Ptolemys were foreign rulers of latter-day Egypt), were to be found in the hieroglyphic upper text enclosed by the oval, so-called 'cartouches' thus: ⬭. Thomas Young thought so too and achieved the correct hieroglyph groups for Ptolemy and Berenike in this way. He tried, rather unsuccessfully, to isolate the individual signs that would spell these names. But he did establish some important ground rules for subsequent study: the need, for instance, to read the hieroglyphs starting from the end of the line to which, say, the bird or animal figures of the text faced; the recognition that the Egyptians used some signs, now called determinatives, that do no more than certify, as it were, the meaning of the word or phrase they follow—Young noticed that the names of queens were followed by two hieroglyphs signifying feminity.

With his demotic work, Young was hampered by his not being aware that the Greek text was not exactly translated by the demotic but rather paraphrased. All the same, he was able to make the important suggestions that the demotic was an extreme development of the hieroglyphic and that, consequently, demotic might be no more completely alphabetic than he (correctly) deemed hieroglyphic to be. In the 1820s Young retired from his linguistic works and went back to physics.

Jean-François Champollion, the son of a bookseller in Figeac in the department of Lot, went a long way beyond Young's achievements and so is secure in his place as the real translator of the ancient Egyptian language. He was eleven years old when he met that mathematician, Fourier, who parleyed with the British on board the Foudroyant in Abukir Bay. Fourier was just returned from Egypt in 1801 when he showed the young Champollion some of his papyri and copies of inscriptions he had collected. Champollion seems to have instantly asked whether or not these things could be read and, when he was told they could not, he is reported to have cried 'I shall do it'. At Fourier's, he saw a copy of the Rosetta Stone too.

At 13, Champollion could read Arabic and Coptic, and at 17 he was a member of the faculty of the Lycée at Grenoble. In 1807 he studied with Sylvestre de Sacy and, the next year, decided to start work in earnest on the Rosetta Stone. The work was not to bring full success for a decade and a half, but by 1814 Champollion was already able to make as much, and more, of the demotic inscription as Young could. It is odd to relate, then, that in 1821, two years after Young's exposition in the Encyclopaedia Britannica, Champollion could write that neither hieroglyphic nor demotic were alphabetic at all. Bit by bit, Champollion rapidly shed this view. His work was not helped by the embarrassments that his own and his family's revolutionary and anti-clerical opinions brought on. When Napoleon was removed and the Bourbons restored, Champollion was dismissed from Grenoble University; at least it gave him more time to get on with the study of the hieroglyphs. In this he was undoubtedly aided by Young's prior work. Copies of that same obelisk that Young had studied in Dorset revealed to him that both the names of a Ptolemy and of a Cleopatra were to be found on it. Champollion was able to identify Cleopatra's cartouche by the co-incidence of three signs in it with the same signs in the one of Ptolemy. Ptolemy has in common with Cleopatra P, O, and L. The cartouche of Ptolemy, which Young had already identified, reads thus:

In what Champollion recognized to be Cleopatra's cartouche, three of the same signs occur in more or less their expected places:

The first, third and fourth signs of Ptolemy co-incide with the fifth, fourth and second signs of Cleopatra: P, O, L. Note that we are reading towards the faces of the birds and lions.

Some of the other signs within these two names evidently didn't co-incide exactly: the Greek names must have proved impossible to put directly into the other language on a one-to-one basis of letters corres-ponding. Similar difficulties exist today with the mutual transliteration of, for example, Russian and English words. The Russians have to render Darwin as what is strictly Dar-oo-in and we put a T on the front of Tchaikovsky for which there is no letter present in the Russian original. Champollion realized that the sound after the M of Ptolemy (in Greek 'Ptolemaios', in Egyptian 'Ptolmis') and the sound between the L and O of Cleopatra were being rendered by the same ⟨ in the hieroglyphs. Problematically, the T of Ptolemy and the T of Cleopatra were different signs ⬠ ⬡. Still, as signs 6 and 9 of Cleopatra were the same, they must render the A sound and ⎡ must then be an S on the end of Ptolemy (in accordance with the Greek original Ptolemaios). Champollion already knew from Young that ⎔ was the feminine determinative

56

at the end of Cleopatra's name. He went on to spot Alexander (Alksentrs) because it had six of his known signs and he guessed the others as K, N and another S. As Young had done, he got out Berenike by knowing all but two of its letters and again noting its feminine determinative at the end of its cartouche corresponding with the name in the Greek text. So he learned the hieroglyphs for B and another form of K.

Thomas Young visited Champollion in 1822 and found him making great progress with the encartouched foreign names despite his anti-alphabetical stand of the previous year. Champollion was soon able to read a great many Greek and Roman names on the Rosetta Stone, the Kingston Lacey obelisk and other late-period inscriptions. This was the stage that he had reached when he wrote his famous letter to M. Dacier, the secretary of the Academy of Inscriptions, which first announced his successes. The letter went on to arouse a little complaint because it extended to Young only the same acknowledgement of his work on the demotic that it conceded to de Sacy and Åkerblad. The most it says about Young's contributions to the study of the hieroglyphs is to describe them as 'analogous'. Like Young, in any case, Champollion at this stage clung to the view that the only phonetic use to which the ancient Egyptians might have put their hieroglyphs was reserved for rendering foreign names. This was a case of 'festina lente', with Champollion edging his way by small steps towards his great breakthrough.

On the 14th of September, 1822, just after publishing his letter to M. Dacier, Champollion took his next step as he studied a newly-copied text, far older than the Graeco-Roman period material he had confined himself to so far, from Abu Simbel in the far south of Egypt—the temple recently saved from the waters of the new lake Nasser. Champollion came upon these signs within a cartouche:

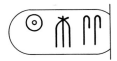

Now he knew that �𓏤 was SS and he had already surmised (not quite correctly) that 𓄿 was an M. He next made the imaginative leap of conjecturing that ⊙ represented the sun and, through the Coptic 'Re' for sun, that its value was that of the sun-god's name known from the classical writers, 'Ra'. RA—M—SS: this must be the Ramesses of Manetho's king-list. Champollion had now allowed the ancient Egyptians to have used their hieroglyphs phonetically not just for foreign names but for their own Egyptian names too. What was more, recalling his knowledge of Coptic again, he was able to see that 𓄿 was not M but MS which he knew to possess the same meaning in Coptic—*and presumably in ancient*

57

Egyptian too—as, say, the Gaelic 'Mac', 'son of'. Ramesses—'son of the sun' (god). Thothmes, Tuthmosis in Greek, soon followed: 'the son of the (god) Thoth':

At a stroke, Champollion had come to realize that the hieroglyphs were not phonetically employed merely to render foreign names or even Egyptian names, they rendered the working of a real language through and through. In his hands, his knowledge of Coptic could now proceed to reveal to him the meanings of any and all parts of the ancient Egyptian texts as words pure and simple, the rational written records of a real language and not arcane holy symbols. Wholesale translation was now a possibility.

Without Coptic, even though it had departed so very far from ancient Egyptian (and Champollion's labours gradually revealed to him how far that was), the Rosetta Stone might not have been of so much help so soon—we are still in the position of being able to pronounce, but not read the meaning of, Etruscan, lacking as we do the first hint of its affinity with any known language.

As he went on with his work of translation, Champollion came to appreciate more and more clearly that hieroglyphs are no more entirely alphabetic than entirely pictographic. There were many complications, with sometimes two signs for the same Greek letter as we have seen. Coptic turned out to have deviated much further than he at first thought from ancient Egyptian and he could now see that the late hieroglyphs of the Rosetta Stone were not the best guide to the older and more 'classical' inscriptions.

In 1824 he published his 'Précis du système hiéroglyphique', which is his first full statement that the hieroglyphs not only render foreign names, not only render kings' names, but render just plain words. For many scholars, the truth of Champollion's claim was immediately obvious. Some however—not Young himself—complained of his plagiarizing Young's work. Some decried his whole system as charlatanry. A German who went to live in the United States kept up a long opposition to Champollion and the professor of Hebrew at Trinity College, Dublin, denounced Young and Champollion as downright impious in going against scripture as he saw it. Only when the Prussian Karl Richard Lepsius wrote to Champollion's student Rossellini in 1837 that Champollion's system was the one true light, and then went on to find another bi-lingual 'Rosetta Stone'—the 'Decree of Canopus', was the matter really settled. By then Champollion, who had exerted himself mightily in his work on the Egyptian language and during an expedition to Egypt and in his newly created post of professor of Egyptology at the Collège de France, had been dead for five years. He was only 42. Lepsius and Charles de Rougé, who eventually followed Champollion to his chair of Egyptology, and another German, Karl Heinrich Brugsch (and later Maspero, Erman, Sethe and Gardiner), were the men who took the study of the language on from where Champollion had left it. It fell to them to discover how complicated this ancient language really was, which persisted historically from 3000 BC until the early centuries AD in an ever-evolving and changing way until it became the Coptic of the Christian Egyptians.

It is worth recognizing at this stage a problem that faces the layman over the Egyptian language. That is the multiplicity of renderings encountered in the literature of Egyptology. We find Tutankhamen and Tutankhamun, for example, and Akhenaten and Akhnaton, Ikhnaton and (in German) Echnaton. These variants have arisen because we simply do not know the exact pronunciation values of the ancient signs. From Coptic, from Greek versions, from the cuneiform renderings of Egyptian words by the Mesopotamians, from the way the ancient Egyptians handled foreign words for themselves we can arrive at useful approximations. But we have to admit that pronunciation changed through the three thousand years of Egyptian history, that vowel sounds were not singly represented by the Egyptians (any more than the Arabic-speaking modern Egyptians lay great stress on vowel values) and that sound-values were almost certainly modified in accordance with different positions within a word or phrase. Superimposed on all of that is a European scholarly tradition of using the Greek forms of various names and words—like Amenophis for Amenhotep (or Amenhetep or Amenhotpe) or Osiris for something like Usir; at least this has the merit of offering versions we can all agree upon, but it does not, of course, cover very many cases.

Champollion's decipherment made it possible for the multitude of texts and inscriptions from ancient Egypt to be understood. The result of this was not, perhaps, immediately to revolutionize the study of Egyptology in the way that might have been hoped.

A good many of the more obvious inscriptions, posted up all over temple walls, have a formulaic character of official or sacerdotal dullness and repetitiveness that could not readily advance the scholars' aims. Even with the language understood, Egyptology had to some extent still to await the enlightenment that only proper archaeology could offer, if only in the course of bringing to light some of the papyrus treasures of ancient Egypt.

Archaeology, as the systematic study of all that the surviving remains of the past can tell us, did not spring up overnight in Egypt; but neither did it only gradually evolve out of the casual investigations of the early travellers and explorers. We can identify three steps towards the establishment of at least the idea of proper archaeology in Egypt (obviously poor excavation technique did not stop the moment the real thing began) and these three steps are associated with the personalities of three preeminent figures in the history of Egyptology.

The first phase, in the person of Giovanni Battista Belzoni, is really perhaps only what had happened before writ large. Belzoni shared many of the attitudes of those European travellers and adventurers who were coming to Egypt in the early part of the nineteenth century with an eye on taking away with them when they left some little—and frequently large—memento of their travels. After Napoleon's forces had quit Egypt, the British did not attempt to take the place over for themselves but rather helped the Turks to reassert their rule there. But once again the Turks were content to install a 'pasha' who would run the country nominally as part of the Ottoman Empire but really with a free hand so long as he kept up the tax-flow back into the Sultan's coffers. In 1805, this role fell to the amazing Albanian adventurer Mohamed Ali. This soldier of fortune had grown up in the medieval atmosphere of the Ottoman Empire but his genius made him eager to modernize the run-down Egypt he had taken in charge: it is possible that, had this ambition not failed to square with British interests, he might have taken on the whole shaky Empire of the Turks in the same spirit.

In his determination to modernize Egypt, Mohamed Ali was anxious to attract western specialists of all sorts to his side. If allowing the foreigners to make off with little bits and pieces, or big bits and pieces, of the archaeological heritage of his domain would help to bring them over, then Mohamed Ali was content to give away these things. One European visitor is supposed to have remarked to him that: 'I am convinced that one may not properly present oneself in Europe on return from Egypt without having a mummy in one hand and a crocodile in the other'. And so the trafficking in antiquities began on a grand scale—at first largely in the hands of Armenians and Greeks, rather than of the Egyptians themselves. Mohamed Ali let it prosper for the sake of opening up his country to the modern world. It was in this way that Belzoni came to Egypt.

Belzoni was recruited by the colourfully named agent of Mohamed Ali in Istanbul, Captain Ishmael Gibraltar. The idea was that Belzoni, something of an expert on hydraulics, should go to Egypt to interest the pasha in a device for pumping water more efficiently than oxen alone could do. Apparently Belzoni successfully demonstrated his invention, but Mohamed Ali turned it down. By then, however, Belzoni was in Egypt. He had had a chequered career. He had been in a monastery for some years in Italy and he had been a circus-strongman in England: as the 'Patagonian Sampson' he had carried a human pyramid of twelve men around the stage at Sadler's Wells in 1803, 'in a manner never attempted by any but himself'. Hydraulics had played some part in his magician's

Above *Before it was toppled and broken,
this figure of Ramesses II was probably
the largest-ever statue in ancient Egypt.
It is supposed to have inspired Shelley's
poem about Ozymandias, King of Kings.*

Right *A pioneering 'Egyptologist', the
former circus-strongman, Belzoni, was
the first explorer (and looter) of many
famous Egyptian monuments.*

shows but he seems certainly to have possessed real skill and knowledge as an engineer. In England this 6′7″ giant had married an Englishwoman who went with him to Egypt.

In Egypt, Belzoni fell in with the British consul-general, Henry Salt, who was busy—for financial gain—in looting antiquities for shipping back to patrons in England. Salt hired Belzoni to go up the Nile to Thebes and bring back a great head of Ramesses II that was lying in the sand in his mortuary temple on the West Bank of the river, so that it could be passed on to Alexandria and Salt's patrons at the British Museum. It was a formidable task to shift the head and load it onto a barge, but it stands in the Egyptian gallery of the British Museum today, thanks to Belzoni. An even larger head-and-shoulders of Ramesses still lies toppled in his Ramesseum, a plausible candidate for the prototype of Shelley's Ozymandias:

> I met a traveller from an antique land
> Who said: Two vast and trunkless legs of stone
> Stand in the desert. Near them on the sand,
> Half sunk, a shatter'd visage lies, whose frown
> And wrinkled lip and snear of cold command
> Tell that its sculptor well those passions read
> Which yet survive, stamp'd on these lifeless things,
> The hand that mock'd them and the heart that fed;
> And on the pedestal these words appear:
> "My name is Ozymandias, king of kings:
> Look on my works, ye Mighty, and despair!"
> Nothing beside remains. Round the decay
> Of that colossal wreck, boundless and bare,
> The lone and level sands stretch far away.

Ozymandias is a Greek attempt to render User-maat-re, another of Ramesses' names, and Shelley knew the claim of the classical writer Diodorus Siculus that in his time an inscription read: 'My name is Ozymandias, King of Kings, if any would know how great I am . . . let him surpass me in any of my works!'

Belzoni never despaired of his ability and right to shift even the most imposing of ancient Egyptian monuments. Nor, evidently, can he ever have heard of the curse of the pharaohs. Here is his description of a tomb-ransacking incident: 'I sought a resting place and found one; but when my weight bore on the body of an Egyptian, it crushed it like a band-box. I naturally had recourse to my hands to sustain my weight, but they found no better support; so that I sank altogether among the broken mummies, with the crash of bones, rags and wooden cases, which raised such a dust as kept me motionless for a quarter of an hour'. And again: 'Every step

I took I crushed a mummy in some part or other'. Belzoni performed prodigious feats of exploration and excavation in Egypt, but he was not an archaeologist: he undertook his work in order to make the grossest and most obvious assessments of the places he was investigating and, if possible, to loot away something spectacular for his backers; a touch of the showman lingers on in his 'Exhibition' in London in 1819 (the year that Young's Encyclopaedia Britannica article appeared) and it is clear that he cared less for the historical meaning of his finds than for these objects as 'objets'. His sometime patron, Henry Salt, was just another such, who had a great rival-in-looting of exactly his own mind, his opposite number in the French consulate, Bernardino Drovetti. Drovetti, Piedmontese by birth, had been a colonel with Napoleon in Egypt. He was a born pillager, and Salt and Drovetti were bound to be rivals: it is said that, as a sort of honour among thieves, these two carved up Egypt between them (rather as the Pope had divided South America for the Spanish and Portuguese) with Salt reputedly getting everything on the left bank and Drovetti everything on the right! They put up the local Arab leaders all over Egypt to see off anyone else who tried to get in on the looting. Once they quarrelled, at Karnak, over an obelisk that Belzoni was bringing down from Philae for Salt, each laying claim to it and with the added complication that Salt had already conceded it to another Englishman. The English claim won out in the end, but only after Belzoni had had an unpleasant confrontation—at which shots were fired—with Drovetti's gang. Mr. Bankes got his obelisk: it is the one that he had already copied to the benefit of Young and Champollion and that now weathers in Dorset.

The late 1830s mark the beginnings of a transition to the next phase of the development of real archaeology in Egypt. An American, George Gliddon (the first American consul in Cairo), was among the earliest to raise voice against the wholesale pillaging of the Egyptian past. In his lectures around America he constantly complained that if things went on like this, the antiquities of Egypt would soon be scattered all over the world and unavailable for serious study. An officer of Wellington's, Richard Howard Vyse, teamed up at about this time with a civil engineer working for Mohamed Ali, John Perring, to investigate the pyramids. They worked, in this archaeologically transitional period, with some knowledge of the hieroglyphs behind them and with the definite aim of advancing knowledge as much as satisfying mere curiosity, but that they too were not yet proper archaeologists is demonstrated by Vyse's fruitless but damaging attempt to blast his way into the smallest of the three Giza pyramids, the one he correctly identified as belonging to Mycerinus. In the end he found his way in rather easily by removing stones loosened by the Arabs during their attempt—at the whim of an emir of the Middle Ages—to demolish the thing entirely, an enterprise which gained little

63

Above *Mohamed Ali, the modernizing ruler of Egypt in the first half of the nineteenth century, promoted archaeology as a way to interest the wide world in his country.*

Above left *Auguste Mariette was the first to take action against the plundering of ancient Egyptian monuments —he himself unearthed the magnificent statue of Chephren that now graces the Cairo Museum.*

Left *Flinders Petrie almost single-handedly founded the science of Egyptology.*

success for over a year's work. Some of the original granite casing-blocks of this pyramid are still in place at the base. Vyse's entry revealed that once again the robbers of old had got the goods, but the sarcophagus did contain some human bones. The chances are that these are not of Mycerinus, but belong to a later intruded burial. Having survived after a fashion the would-be demolition of the Arabs and the blasting of Vyse, Mycerinus' legacy was to suffer one more indignity: his stone sarcophagus (a fine one to judge from old sketches) was put on board ship at Alexandria bound for the British Museum; after Leghorn, the ship foundered and Mycerinus' sarcophagus still lies somewhere off the Mediterranean coast of Spain.

Mohamed Ali does seem to have appreciated that such large-scale depletions of the cultural coffers of his country were not in its ultimate best interests, but he did nothing very exacting to reduce either the trafficking in antiquities or the more scholarly depradations of university expeditions from Europe so long as he thought that it all encouraged the modernization of Egypt. Who is to say that he was wrong in that? It fell to a Frenchman, a quarter of a century later, during the rule of one of Mohamed Ali's successors, to see clearly the need to do something official about stopping the losses. Auguste Ferdinand Mariette is the figure on whom the second phase of the development of responsible archaeology pivots. He was not himself a very good 'field' archaeologist by later standards but he did bring to the study a conscience about what was being done to the antiquities of Egypt that achieved a concrete expression in the setting up of the 'Service d'Antiquités'. Mariette was a big and enthusiastic man who had been filling the less-than-fulfilling post at the Louvre of assistant curator, cataloguing papyri, for ten years when he was sent off to Egypt by the Museum in 1850, principally to buy papyri and Coptic manuscripts but also—in a clause that Mariette was to exploit to the full—to look into general antiquities. In other words, he was sent to buy loot. When he got to Egypt, Mariette found that the Coptic patriarch had been caught before by European manuscript-hunters and was now greatly on his guard against them. This fortunate thwarting of Mariette's mission led him to turn his attention elsewhere. In any case, he fell in love with Egypt almost at first sight and began to work up a moral and scholarly outrage of his own at what he saw of the trafficking in antiquities that was to issue eventually in his bold attempt to close down all excavations in the country that were not under his control.

His first great discovery came in 1851, when—forsaking papyri and manuscripts—he used his finances from the Louvre to uncover the great Serapaeum complex that the old classical geographer Strabo had mentioned as the site of the worship—in ancient Egypt's decline—of the latter-day god Serapis. Mariette had noticed in Alexandria, and went on noting in Cairo, that it was common to find modern villas fronted with what

were obviously old sphinx statues, those human- (and usually male-) headed lion figures. Obviously these things were coming from some ancient site in some abundance, and he remembered that Strabo's Serapaeum had been avenued with sphinxes which were already up to their necks in sand in his day. Using his Louvre resources to hire a big team of workmen, he eventually uncovered one hundred and forty more sphinxes at Sakkara, the ancient necropolis about 25 kilometres west of Cairo. They were indeed part of the Serapaeum complex, and he went on to find inside its rock-cut galleries the remains of the embalmed burials of bulls in great stone sarcophagi. Very importantly for the study of the ancient Egyptian chronology, he also found some five hundred 'stelae' (inscribed plaques) commemorating bull-burials and ceremonies at the Serapaeum that took place during the reigns of pharaohs from the time of Amenophis III (about 1400 BC) down to very late times. Though some might complain at Mariette's use of his funds for purposes of excavation, the importance of the find established his place in Egypt and, as for himself, he was completely committed now. In later years he used to warn those who expressed an interest in dabbling in Egyptology that the bug was a fatal one that could not be resisted once it bit, and many since have discovered the truth of that warning.

In 1857, with the backing of Ferdinand de Lesseps of Suez Canal fame, Mariette was appointed by Said Pasha, the then khedive of Egypt, to the post of conservator of Egyptian monuments. He was now in a position to act against the looters. He was absolutely determined that Egyptian antiquities of all sorts should henceforth cease to be taken out of the country but should stay in Egypt in their proper place as the cultural birthright of the modern nation where they could be studied and appreciated in a way that their dispersal across Europe and America would make impossible. Mariette went about implementing this determination a little obsessively perhaps (no doubt that was necessary, for it was a long time before the depredations were brought under complete control), and his concern to stop unqualified excavation led him to try and do all the major work himself. He was not the world's best excavator and his wide-ranging investigations meant that he could not always keep a proper eye on what was being done in his name. He was not, moreover, very prompt at writing up the results of his work—a not unknown failing among the professionals in all branches of archaeology to this day. Nevertheless his achievement, quite apart from his key role in putting down the looting, is enormous: he dug at Karnak, Abydos, Abu Simbel, Tanis in the Delta; he cleared out the temple at Edfu and had a disfiguring Arab village removed from its roof; he discovered the temple associated with the Chephren pyramid (we now know that most pyramids have temples) and in it unearthed the fine statue of Chephren now in the Cairo Museum; he supplied the story for Verdi's 'Aida', which opened the Cairo

Opera House in 1869 (sadly burned down in 1972) at the time of the inauguration of the Suez Canal. He died in 1881, and is buried in a granite and marble tomb outside the Cairo Museum.

At the close of Mariette's Egyptological rule, archaeology of all sorts—both prehistoric and historical—had begun to take on its modern shape and role. The archaeology of the other ancient civilizations had come a long way: the Assyrians had been revived with Rawlinson's heroic work on the great tri-lingual inscription at Behistun between Iraq and Iran; Schliemann had discovered, if not Homer's Troy, then a whole series of Troys near the mouth of the Dardanelles; and towards the southern end of the Tigris-Euphrates delta the first indications were coming to light of a whole civilization that had been almost entirely lost to view, the 'land of Shinar' of the Bible, which we know as Sumer. Biblical enthusiasm was a great motor of the study of early civilizations, a fundamentalist backlash against the devastations of Darwinism, and it is interesting to note the first intentions of the Egypt Exploration Fund set up in England in 1882 (and still proudly flourishing as the Egypt Exploration Society): 'to organize expeditions in Egypt, with a view to the elucidation of the History and Arts of Ancient Egypt and the illustration of the Old Testament narrative, so far as it has to do with Egypt and the Egyptians'. The Swiss-born Henri Naville was a chief excavator on behalf of the Fund, but another digger who benefited early from its support was the man who marks the third stage in the development of Egyptian archaeology, the figure with whom the subject achieves the standing of real, sound archaeology: William Matthew Flinders Petrie. With Gaston Maspero, the Frenchman who succeeded Mariette as director of the Service, and Johann Peter Adolf Erman the brilliant, if rather more arm-chair, German Egyptologist, Flinders Petrie belongs to the trio who formed and dominated Egyptology around the turn of the century. But Flinders Petrie was the methodologist of the actual field practice of archaeology and so the most important for an understanding of the establishment of the subject.

Flinders Petrie arrived in Egypt on what was something of a fool's errand. In 1880 his father encouraged him to go there in pursuance of one of his own addictions: to the cranky notions of the Scottish Astronomer Royal, Charles Piazzi Smyth, who thought that the Great Pyramid of Cheops at Giza enshrined a divinely ordained system of weights and measures for all time, including his famous 'pyramid inch'. Whether or not the young Flinders Petrie, who had measured Stonehenge for similar reasons, already considered Piazzi Smyth's ideas to be the nonsense they are, he soon found that Smyth was not even basing himself on accurate measurements and abandoned the whole theory. He did however persist with his own accurate survey. The stories about his long career in Egyptology are many and sometimes no doubt apocryphal: from his pyramid-survey

The so-called 'Village Headman' (named for its likeness
to a local sheik at the time of
its finding) is in fact the
statue of a dignitary named
Ka-aper of the Fifth Dynasty,
around 2400 BC. Against
the common reputation of
Egyptian art, the piece is
clearly an extremely 'realistic'
rendering of an individual
man.

The dry climate of Egypt has preserved a substantial amount of wooden material to set alongside the stone monuments. Hesi-re was a noble of the Third Dynasty (about 2700 BC) whose tomb included scenes carved on wooden panels depicting the dead but eternal man to the accompaniment of some finely carved hieroglyphic inscriptions.

days comes the one about his scandalizing lady tourists at Giza by appearing in the entrance of the pyramid clad only in long combinations— it is hot work exerting oneself inside the Great Pyramid.

The thing that made Petrie's attitude to archaeology so strikingly different from and more rewarding than that of virtually everyone who preceded him (and a few successors) was that he was not fascinated by the fine and beautiful things he found to the neglect of the seemingly dull and everyday. He cherished everything from which he could extract information. Perhaps there is something about the high incidence of 'belles pièces' among the relics of great civilizations like the Egyptian one (or the Greek) that makes it inevitable that in the early days of their archaeological study all eyes will be fixed upon only the finest and most aesthetically rewarding finds. Certainly this was true of Egypt—perhaps only the Scotsman Alexander Rhind had, before Flinders Petrie, any notion of the importance of the commonplace. An instance of the success of Petrie's attitude is afforded at Abydos. The French abbé Amélineau had worked over the great cemeteries at Abydos at the end of the nineteenth century, looking for fine pieces and disregarding everything else. Petrie came to the site in 1890 when the abbé considered it quite exhausted and, working with the discarded broken pots and other inconsiderables of Amélineau, he was able to make this unprepossessing stuff brilliantly illuminate the earliest historical days of Egypt, the time of the previously quite shadowy First and Second Dynasties.

Petrie liked to dig a site a year and consequently got the first look in on many of the best archaeological sites in Egypt which have subsequently been re-worked by those who came after him (many of whom he trained). He recorded his finds meticulously and used photography as an aid. He published with admirable promptness. At Nakada, he investigated—and not only investigated, but recorded—three thousand graves in one season, collecting a mass of material that turned out to belong to the Predynastic Period.

The latter half of the nineteenth century was the time of the great success of Charles Darwin's work in establishing the idea of evolution. The idea bit deep and was applied outside natural history. It had an obvious archaeological application, because it offered the archaeologist faced, for instance, with masses of different sorts of axe from different levels in a site or different sites, the possibility of ordering them in a sequence of development, running perhaps from what one judged to be the simplest to the most elaborate. General Pitt Rivers in England went from ordering his fire-arm collection in this way to making sense of his collection of stone and metal tools from archaeological sites on the same principle. Of course, one did not have to be too simple-minded about these schemes: a type might also degenerate, from the fully practical to the simply symbolic for example.

One such case suggested itself to Flinders Petrie with his vast Nakada collections. In general, Egyptian sites do not display the complex stratigraphy of layers seen elsewhere that can reveal the evolution of types through time as the archaeologist comes up towards present-day ground level: Egyptian sites are just swamped in sand. Petrie remarked that some of the groups of associated finds from some particular graves at Nakada resembled what he knew to be things from the earliest dynasties of Egypt. How could the rest of the graves be ordered in a sequence that would reflect their relative ages? There was found to occur in a good many graves, though not constant in form, a particular sort of pot with two wavy handles. These pots were not always identical, and so raised the possibility of being ordered on a sort of evolutionary scale. In what Petrie assumed to be the latest graves, the ones as a whole most like the early dynastic finds, these pots really had no handles at all but only a token-apology for a pair of handles in the form of decorative scrolls. This could be viewed as a degenerating sequence and Petrie went ahead and ordered these wavy-handled pots in the light of that notion, with the fully practical, boldly-handled ones at the beginning. It was entirely plausible that a pot form that once needed proper handles should, in a spirit of conservatism, be kept on with increasingly perfunctory handles after, perhaps, its usefulness had changed. It was possible for Petrie to extend the assumption with his graves by observing that another pot-form, decorated in red, co-incided with the early wavy-handled ones and also occurred on its own without them at a presumably earlier date, while some attractive red pots with black mouths co-incided with some, but not all, of the red decorated ones but never when the wavy-handled ones were present and so these red and black ones when they occurred on their own must mark their graves as earlier still. This was Petrie's famous 'sequence dating' which—while it did not give an *absolute* date in years—made it possible to arrive at a *relative* chronology for these pot-forms and the graves they came from. As a final scrupulous touch, Petrie started his sequence at the arbitrary figure of 30 (running to 80) so that if any even earlier pot-forms turned up in some other graves they could be accommodated on the scale.

Of course, when all the rest of the associations of pots and flints and/or copper tools and/or figures and so on were taken into account (Flinders Petrie did not consider items in isolation, but as components of groups of associated finds), a very versatile framework for dating subsequent finds from this period could be worked out—even if only a knife turned up on its own. Flinders Petrie's sequence dating still has its uses, but its chief significance today is that it shows what a different sort of attitude was now being brought to bear on the archaeology of Egypt and how enormously rewarding both in detail and in principle this new attitude could be.

Flinders Petrie was a very single-minded and determined man, to the point of eccentricity. Stories about him are even now current Egyptological gossip: like his predeliction, forced upon his collaborators, for tinned peas as the best all round diet for busy diggers; tinned peas might be served, from the can, with unrelenting monotony throughout a season. But it is certain that his rigour and high standards in field archaeology, coupled with his respect for the total range of surviving evidence as material for scientific investigation, put Egyptian archaeology into its modern frame of mind and laid the groundwork for its subsequent successes.

Chapter IV   Egyptian History
in the Ancient World:
to the End
of the Old Kingdom

An historical framework is a necessary aid to the understanding of any civilization. It is frustrating and misleading not to know where various aspects and features fit into the whole picture of the course of an ancient civilization in particular. Moreover, in the case of Egypt, there is always the danger that the very conservatism and 'Egyptian-ness' of the civilization in question will create a temptation to regard it in an ahistorical spirit, overemphasizing those static and timeless qualities that the Egyptians themselves so valued to the neglect of the real historical developments and changes that this society experienced. One of the powerful reasons why ancient Egypt has attracted so much obscurantist speculation arises out of the easy possibility of treating it in an undynamic and non-developmental way. Like every other society in every other time and place, ancient Egypt has a history of political, social, religious and artistic development and it is essential to be familiar with the broad outlines of the historical framework to which these changes belong.

Another danger inherent in the study of the ancient Egyptian civilization comes about because of the very distinctiveness and isolated quality of the culture of the Nile Valley. Ancient Egypt tends very easily to assume a 'sui generis' appearance without reference to the rest of the ancient world. There is considerable justification for this, particularly in Old Kingdom times when the country was largely self-sufficient and without extensive foreign involvements—though even in those days trade and commercial contacts were definitely present. In Middle Kingdom times, and especially during the New Kingdom, ancient Egypt's international dealings were very extensive, so much so that the blame for some major changes in Egyptian society can be laid at the door of the foreign involvements in which the empire found itself entangled.

The arrangement of Egyptian history into 'dynasties' is owed to Manetho, that native-born Egyptian priest of the time of the first Ptolemaic rulers, around 300 BC. His thirty dynasties from Menes to the conquest of Alexander have proved useful enough to be retained by the generations of modern Egyptologists, though with inevitable modifications, and there is now little or no prospect of the dynastic framework's being abandoned by Egyptology. Accordingly it is as well to be familiar with the system, if only to be able to orientate oneself quickly when references occur to this and that dynasty. Manetho wrote in Greek and gave Graecized names to the rulers he enumerated. These are not always the same as the Greek forms adopted by Herodotus: for example, Herodotus' Min is Manetho's Menes, Manetho's Mencheres is Herodotus' Mycerinus. At first sight, it might seem that the Graecizing of the ancient Egyptian names is a nuisance and a distraction and many might wish to have the real Egyptian usages in preference to foreign versions. In fact, the Greek forms are something of a blessing for the simple reason, already mentioned, that we do not know in the vast majority of cases how the ancient Egyptian words were pronounced. It is now generally thought best, therefore, to employ the Greek forms of those ancient names where the Greek forms exist and do not depart too far from the true consonant-structure that can be read in the hieroglyphic prototypes. For this reason Tuthmosis is preferred to Thothmes, and Cheops to Khufu. But for a considerable number of ancient Egyptian names no Greek equivalents exist, and we are obliged to employ reconstructions of the original Egyptian, with vowels inserted on the Coptic pattern to make these names more palatable than a mere spelling out of their consonant skeletons would leave them. Sometimes this 'Egyptian' form has achieved too wide a currency for an admittedly extant Greek rendering to be acceptable: here the generalissimo who succeeded Tutankhamun will be called Horemheb and not Harmäis.

Egyptian chronology has always been a problem, though perhaps no more so than that of other very ancient civilizations who did not objectively reckon their history in the absolute terms of the passage of years and whose own annals have not survived intact. The ancient Egyptians created several historical accounts of their own civilization that have come down to us in only fragmentary form. Instead of telling us that such and such an event occurred in, say, AD 1939 or 1317 of the Muslim calendar, the ancient Egyptian annals record a happening of, say, year 9 of the reign of this or that pharaoh. The number of years that a given king ruled were listed in these records and sometimes totals for a set of rulers, as in the case of Manetho's account. If these ancient annals and histories had survived intact and if they were altogether trustworthy accounts of what had gone on, then there would be no doubts as to the chronology of ancient Egypt. Unfortunately, the concept of an objective recording of past events was not uppermost in the minds of these pioneer 'historians', who sometimes re-ordered or eliminated the reigns of un-favoured rulers (rather in the manner of the Soviet Encyclopedia), and in any case their works have come down to us only in a damaged, excerpted and fragmentary state. The full texts of Manetho's original work presumably went up in flames when the library of Alexandria was burned down in the time of Caesar, if it had not already perished. Variant excerpts of his 'Egyptian Memoirs' are given by Josephus, the Romanized Jewish historian, and in the writings of early Christians like Africanus and Eusebius. His transmitters do differ in their retailing of his work, and where they agree then the original is sometimes plainly inaccurate as with cases like that of the Amarna heretic king Akhenaten and his successors. Still, what is left of Manetho is a very useful guide.

In addition to him, there are four other important king-lists and annals, as well as the table of some fifty kings inscribed on a temple wall at Karnak during the reign of Tuthmosis III in about 1450 BC. This latter is less useful because strict chronological order was not the aim here. The Palermo Stone—whose largest known fragment resides in the Sicilian capital, and of which (or of another identical original) most of the remaining pieces are in Cairo—was an account of the kings of Egypt and the principal events of their reigns from late predynastic days down to the Fifth Dynasty of Old Kingdom times. Unfortunately, the name of Menes himself would lie in the broken-off area and the stone has none of the chronological usefulness it would have possessed had it survived intact. The Turin Canon of kings is a papyrus from the reign of Ramesses II, around 1250 BC, written in the hieratic cursive style and sadly surviving only in some fifty small pieces. It was discovered early on in the history of Egyptology and handled (some think man-handled!) by the French agent Drovetti. Champollion himself wrestled with these fragments. Since then ingenious scholarship has reconstituted it as well as may be but it remains very incomplete. Like Manetho's account, it begins with Menes (both precede him with the names of the divine and semi-divine rulers of Egypt before the first human dynasty), and then goes on to list his successors with both considerable agreement with and divergences from Manetho. The stone-cut Table of Sakkara, also from the reign of Ramesses II (it occurs in the tomb of an overseer of works) lists about fifty kings but for reasons unknown does not start until half-a-dozen after Menes. From the reign of Ramesses II's father, Sethos I (Seti I) comes the Table of Abydos showing the king and his son making offerings to seventy-six of their royal forebears, in the form of their encartouched names, beginning again with Menes. Apart from Manetho, then, there is no ancient Egyptian historical list that comes down later than the reign of Ramesses II around 1250 BC though the records of a family of priests claiming long-term service does extend into later times. Of course, for later times the study of the other civilizations of the ancient world and their commercial and military dealings with Egypt helps greatly to fix the course of events in Egypt itself: by the time of Ramesses II extensive foreign involvements were the order of the day and this situation was maintained down to the end of independent Egyptian history. Because of this, both the order of events in Egypt from late New Kingdom times onwards and their absolute chronology in terms of objective dates can be arrived at with great accuracy.

To reach a remotely comparable situation with regard to the earlier phases of Egyptian history required some very ingenious calculations on the part of the scholars and students of Egyptology. It is interesting to recall that well into this century some authorities—notably Flinders Petrie himself—maintained chronological estimates for ancient Egyptian history that differed widely from the one shortly to be presented here, allowing a much greater age to the early stages of that history. The scheme to be set out here is, however, the one that has achieved widest agreement among scholars over the last forty years or so and it is worth noting that it is the one that best agrees with the radiocarbon dates that have been determined for Egyptian organic remains, particularly since the recent recalibration (involving smallish adjustments in the period that concerns us) of the carbon-14 process.

Happily for modern chronologists, the ancient Egyptians employed a rather inadequate calendar. True to their general conservatism, they moreover resisted attempts to improve it in Ptolemaic times. They contented themselves with a year of 365 days; there were three seasons (called Inundation, Winter and Summer) of four months each; these months were of thirty days and five extra days were added to the year to bring the total up to 365. This falls short of the true astronomical year by just over a quarter of a day. It is clear, therefore, that their formal calendar could in time become completely out of accordance with the real astronomical year. In fact, in 4×365 years, the formal year would go full circle through every permutation of misalignment and arrive back in agreement with the true year. But the Egyptians seem to have early hit upon a device whereby the relationship of the real and the formal year could be easily monitored and New Year's Day determined. The 'going up of Sothis' as they called what astronomers know as the heliacal rising of Sirius was noted to co-incide closely with the beginning of the inundation: after a period of invisibility the dog-star could be observed again just before sunrise at this time of year, and its first appearance was adopted by the Egyptians as their New Year's Day. We know that the real New Year's Day co-incided in AD 139 with the New Year's Day of the formal year—we can be grateful that the calendar had not been reformed in Ptolemaic times, since by counting backwards it is easy to determine that this co-incidence must also have occurred in 1317 BC and 2773 BC. Now there are also re-corded in ancient texts heliacal risings of Sirius at certain times of the formal year during the reign of Tuthmosis III, in year 9 of Amenophis I and year 7 of Sesostris III. By reference back to the known co-incidences of the formal and astronomical years, we may conclude that these dog-star observations were most likely made in the years 1469, 1536 and 1872 BC. Here we have the beginnings of a chronological framework for ancient Egyptian history.

If the reign of Sesostris III includes the year 1872 BC, then inscriptional evidence puts that of Ammenemes I (the first king of the Twelfth Dynasty) at about 1990 BC. To the preceding Eleventh Dynasty, the Turin Canon allots 143 years (which seems reasonable: the actual numbers of years each for four of the six reigns of that dynasty have survived, totalling 120 and we know that the other two reigns were short). This puts the end of the First Intermediate Period, which preceded the Eleventh Dynasty, back to about 2100 BC. The length of this period must be guessed at between a hundred to two hundred years: there were a lot of rulers, but none ruled for long and sometimes several more or less simultaneously. If we judge that this First Intermediate Period began in about 2250 BC and accept Manetho's assertion that the kings from the First Dynasty to the end of the Sixth ruled for about a thousand years, then the rule of Menes and the beginning of dynastic history must be placed at around 3100 BC, give or take a hundred years perhaps. Manetho's claim is, on average, reasonable for that period since archaeology has disclosed the remains of roughly the same number of rulers as he and the rest of the king-lists suggest and this figure of about 50 divided into his thousand years allows about 20 years to each ruler. Some reigns were longer of course, and some perhaps very short but the average is plausible. Let it be noted that an attempt to shift all the early phases of Egyptian history back by another 4×365 years would lead to an unplausibly long and uneventful chronology that would not well agree with the rest of world history and would certainly contradict the radiocarbon dates.

Ancient Egypt's is an *historical* civilization illuminated by the evidence of written annals from its later phases, considerable bodies of literature from its middle period on, and some scraps of written material from its very earliest days. None the less, for those earliest days and indeed up until its middle period, it is not primarily written records but *archaeology* that furnishes us with what we know about its course and character. In the outline of Egyptian history that follows, it should be remembered that archaeology holds sway over the Archaic and (for the most part) the Old Kingdom phases while written records become more and more important from Middle Kingdom times.

Archaic Period c3100–2750 BC First and Second Dynasties
Manetho's Dynasties I to VI are nowadays grouped together as 'the Old Kingdom'. Of these, Dynasties I and II are referred to as 'the Archaic Period'. It is a period of great obscurity and difficulties of archaeological interpretation. Traditionally Manetho's Menes, called Meni in the Turin

78

and Abydos lists, stands at its head. Herodotus rendered him as Min and tells us that he founded the city of Memphis on land that he reclaimed from marsh by diverting the course of the Nile for a short distance. This is a very plausible achievement to ascribe to the unifier of Upper and Lower Egypt who must have been a man of great energy and imagination. Herodotus' use of the simple form Min, which in hieroglyphic form would consist only of the letters M and N, is interesting in the light of a couple of archaeological discoveries. The identification of Menes with that king Narmer, whose slate palette shows him on one side in the crown of Upper Egypt and on the other in the Lower Egyptian crown, is perhaps promoted by these bits of evidence. From an Archaic Period site near Abydos, called 'Mother of Pots' in Arabic because of the great quantity of pottery and potsherds found on it, there comes a clay jar-sealing inscribed with the hieroglyphs for Narmer, or Meri-nar if we read them the other way (the 'tent peg' and fish seen at the top of the palette), accompanied by two further hieroglyphs: in fact, the very ones for M and N. The historical kings of Egypt had many titles and names and the rulers of the Archaic Period possessed at least two. One of these, of which Narmer is an example, is called the king's 'Horus-name' and at this early stage it was customary to enclose it in a box-like figure called a 'serekh', which probably represented the façade of the king's palace, surmounted by the falcon of Horus. This name in fact alludes to the king's role, even in the earliest times, as a living incarnation of the ancient Delta falcon-god.

A 'serekh' to enclose a king's name.

At Nakada, but before Flinders Petrie began his own scientific excavations on the site, there was unearthed an ivory docket in 1897 from a great mud-brick tomb. This tomb was a fine example of what are known among Egyptologists as 'mastabas', from an Arabic word that saw in them a resemblance to the low mud benches outside some recent Egyptian houses. The docket would have been attached to a jar or box to identify the owner or donor of its contents. The docket displays the serekh-enclosed Horus-name Aha, and another less orthodox figure wherein, under a vulture and a cobra (symbols of Upper and Lower Egypt that last throughout Egyptian history) and all enclosed by a sort of booth-like structure, there once again occur the letters M and N. The name Aha occurred elsewhere on objects in this ruined tomb and some scholars were led to identify a king of that name with the legendary Menes presumably

79

indicated by the MN. In that case, there would have been the strong possibility that this was indeed the tomb of Menes himself! This engaging theory is eroded by the suggestion that what is depicted here is really Menes' successor Aha conducting some sort of funerary observance before the mortuary booth of his immediately-deceased forerunner. Disappointingly for those who wish to see a ready identification of Narmer with Menes, it has to be pointed out that the seal-impression from the 'Mother of Pots' site may mean only 'Narmer endures', that being the probable correct reading of MN as a verb rather than a name. Since the name Menes itself most likely means 'He who endures', the problem of discerning the nuances of meaning possibly intended by these exiguous scraps of evidence can be seen to be insuperable without more data.

The docket of Aha.

Problems of this sort dog the student through the rest of this First Dynasty and become in some way even greater in the Second. When in the last years of the nineteenth century, Amélineau and then Flinders Petrie investigated the old mastaba tombs at 'Mother of Pots' it seemed likely for well over a quarter of a century that the graves of most if not all of the rulers of the Archaic Period had been discovered. They were robbed out pretty thoroughly and little or nothing remained of the bodies of the kings presumed to have been buried there, but positive identification seemed possible in a number of cases on account of stelae set up in front of the tombs with the names of the kings upon them. Then, between 1935 and his death in 1971, Professor W. B. Emery of London University uncovered at Sakkara a new series of archaic mastabas whose surviving contents frequently carried the names of these same kings whose 'tombs' had already been discovered near Abydos. There were no stelae before these tombs but there were traces of human remains in greater quantity and the tombs themselves were about twice the size of the Abydos ones. Emery concluded that his Sakkara mastabas were the real tombs of the kings of the first two dynasties. In that case, the ones near Abydos became a problem most readily solved by regarding them as 'cenotaphs', empty token-tombs perhaps reflecting the old north-south division of the country and the Upper Egyptian origin of the dynasties that had made their new capital in Memphis. It does seem plausible that the kings who ruled from Memphis should have chosen to be buried nearby, at Sakkara on the desert's edge above the town. Certainly the kings of the Third and Fourth Dynasties were buried close to the capital and, in the case of Djoser's Third Dynasty mortuary complex at Sakkara with its dual pyramid burial-chamber and South Mastaba burial-chamber, there is a known parallel situation, close in time, of a double tomb construction. Perhaps these early rulers, with a strong southern tradition, were providing themselves with tombs in both their Upper and Lower Egyptian domains, so that—at least symbolically—they could continue in death to watch over the Two Lands from two separate burial places. No Sakkara mastaba has been discovered that could be attributed to Menes, however.

There is no literature whatever from the Archaic Period and, indeed, the earliest hieroglyphs are little more than pictograms like those upon the Narmer palette, where a simple sign-picture records the smiting of the marsh dwellers. A progress can be seen towards a more complex use of writing throughout the Archaic period: a small plaquette of ivory in the British Museum shows king Den belabouring an enemy in a manner prototypical of a style that lasted until the end of Egyptian history and the accompanying inscription says quite unmistakably of this deed: 'first time of smiting the Easterners'. They were presumably bedouin of the Sinai region, where the early Egyptians were probably already seeking copper. A fragment of the Palermo Stone mentions king Djer smiting 'Asia'. King Djer is interesting again from the point of view of early foreign relations, since in a hole in the wall of his 'tomb' at Abydos there was found (stuffed in there by robbers?) an arm carrying bracelets with turquoise decorations, traded from somewhere outside Egypt. Whose arm it was is unknown. Djer's name is cut on a rock near the Second Cataract, so he may have campaigned in the south. Certainly some of his successors in the Second Dynasty were trading and fighting quite widely. One king's name was found on a fragment dug up at Byblos, in present-day Lebanon. Even in these early days the Egyptians were probably buying wood there, to ship to the Delta and float down to Memphis. Byblos was already a well-established township, in contact with the Sumerian civilization of Mesopotamia. It went on to become the great Phoenician centre of trade and always played an important role in Egyptian history.

The same king whose name occurs at Byblos is recorded to have built a temple, called 'The Goddess endures' in stone. His own 'tomb' chamber is hewn into stone, and some door jambs from tombs of his time are fashioned in stone too, so that the beginnings of the architectural developments to issue in the great Step Pyramid complex of Djoser of the Third Dynasty can be glimpsed already in the Second.

Though no literature survives from the Archaic Period, the existence of some sort of formulated religious material can be inferred from the more obviously primitive sections of the so-called 'pyramid texts' of the

Fifth Dynasty. These texts were inscribed on the walls of the Wenis Pyramid in particular and some of them do serve to reveal a barbaric tradition that would more properly belong to Archaic times:

'Rise up, o King! Gather up your bones, throw the earth off your flesh, and take up your position at the doors which keep out the common people. The king eats men and lives on gods . . . he consumes their magic; their big ones are for his morning meal, their medium-sized ones are for his evening meal and their old men and old women are for incense to be burnt.'

The primitive impression created by such utterances is re-inforced by some of the evidence that comes both from the Abydos and the Sakkara tomb-fields of the Archaic Period. Associated with the main 'tombs', in a way that clearly points to their having been dug at the same time, are the graves of some numbers of women and practitioners of various professions connected with the court, dwarfs and even perhaps a few high officials. Evidently at this time a tradition of simultaneously burying alongside the dead king the servants of his earthly life was still in force. This resembles the larger-scaled mass funeral sacrifices uncovered at Ur in Mesopotamia and belonging to the Early Dynastic Period there, four or five centuries later than these Egyptian examples. There is no evidence to suggest that in Egypt by 2500 BC (or for that matter a century and a half earlier in the time of the building of the Great Pyramid) this practice of simultaneously burying the servants with the king was still being observed.

The Old Kingdom c2750–2250 BC Third Dynasty 2750–2650 BC
The monuments of the first king of the Third Dynasty constitute the first clear-cut statement of the character of Egyptian civilization. Here, in the Step Pyramid complex at Sakkara, are to be seen all the traits of massive construction in stone, of formalized decoration, of royal pre-eminence and of pre-occupation with eternity. It is salutary to remember, however, that some of the emphasis which the ancient Egyptians seem to us to have put upon the grave and the afterlife is due to the fact that archaeology has been overwhelmingly obliged to base itself upon the tombs these people built high and dry on the desert's edge and out of stone meant to last forever—while their everyday places of work, their homes and even their palaces were made out of perishable mud-brick and wood.

Some pre-figurings of stone construction have been noted in the Second Dynasty; with Djoser's complex the use of stone arrives in a dramatically thoroughgoing way. That these were early days in the use of this new and much more difficult material is demonstrated by the repeated instances where the builders seem to have been looking back over their shoulders to the wooden forms they had previously employed and trying to render these forms in stone rather than strike out immediately into the bold possibilities afforded by the new material. This is usually the way with technological innovations the world over, and not simply due to Egyptian conservatism: our own plastic flower-pots and fibre-glass oaken beams, while perhaps more self-conscious, are not unakin to the uses made of stone in Djoser's monument. And so we can see in the Step Pyramid complex roof-logs carved in stone, wattle fences carved in relief on solid blocks, stone reproductions of half-opened gates and columns engaged in walls rather than trusted to stand on their own. For many people the great complex of Djoser at Sakkara remains the most impressive and affecting of all Egyptian monuments, outdoing the Great Pyramid at Giza or the Hypostyle Hall of columns at Karnak or any of the great tombs in the Valley of the Kings in satisfactoriness of expression and simplicity of statement. Until this century, little but the Step Pyramid itself and a series of irregular mounds could be seen here. Englishmen excavated the site in the first place, but a great debt is owed to Professor J. P. Lauer of Paris for his painstaking restoration work, which continues to this day.

The original architect of the complex was, by tradition (and there is some archaeological evidence to support it), Imhotep, a high official of king Djoser, who was himself deified—among other things as a patron of medicine, a sort of Egyptian Asclepius—in the latter days of Egyptian history.

Whether the great terraced and stairwayed 'ziggurats' of Mesopotamia, whose earliest appearance does pre-date the Egyptian pyramids, had any inspirational influence upon the Egyptians is a problem similar to that of the origin of writing in the two areas. The ziggurats seem to have come into being in the first place as a result of erecting a new shrine on the foundations of an old one; they were brick built and had a shrine on top for the gods. They were not tombs for god-kings and the greatest did not achieve the size of the biggest Egyptian pyramids.

Remembering the problem of the apparent double-tomb provision of the kings of the Archaic Period, it is interesting to see that Djoser himself was provided not only with a burial chamber at the bottom of a shaft under the Step Pyramid but also with another one under a large structure to the south of the pyramid, but still within the enclosure wall of the whole complex, called the South Mastaba. The underground structure of both the pyramid and the South Mastaba is complex and highly decorated, rather in contrast to that of the later pyramids. Presumably, and especially in the light of the southerly placing of the Mastaba (just as Abydos is south of Sakkara), we have here again an effort to endow the dead king with a 'house of eternity' in both Upper and Lower Egypt—at least, in symbolic terms. The Egyptians were great exponents of the idea that to represent a thing is as good as having the thing itself: that is no doubt a universal human tendency, but the Egyptians applied the idea more intensely than most cultures have done. As well as providing Djoser with two tombs, massively constructed to last forever (they are not doing badly) and—we must presume—mummifying his body against corruption, his architect placed at the foot of the northern face of the pyramid a small booth out of which there gazes through two small holes a noble statue of the king, doing duty as a substitute for the king's person to receive the offerings and daily sacrifices that were intended to be made before his tomb.

Another, but unfinished, step pyramid quite similar to Djoser's and believed to be that of a near successor, stands close by at Sakkara. The next stage of pyramid development possibly belongs in part to the last king of the Third Dynasty, called Huni, who may have begun work on the extraordinary collapsed pyramid of Meidum.

Fourth Dynasty 2650–2500 BC

This is the dynasty *par excellence* of pyramid building. Snofru, the first king of this dynasty, seems to have had a hand in at least completing the Meidum Pyramid, whose tower-like appearance has resulted from a collapse following upon an attempt to clothe a step pyramid in a smooth and stepless coat of facing stones. The tower-shape reveals the built-up core of the monument, but when the collapse occurred is not known: it cannot have reached its present state of ruin until over a thousand years later than its construction, since the rubble of its collapse was revealed in Petrie's excavation to have covered up an Eighteenth Dynasty graffito.

Whatever his part in the Meidum enterprise, Snofru seems certainly to have possessed two more pyramids at Dashur, just south of Sakkara. These two again have a north-south distinction and the same ideas about Upper and Lower Egypt may be at work here. The older of the two, the southern one, is called the Bent Pyramid, because—for reasons unknown —its angle of ascent changes about two-thirds of the way up. Probably this reflects experiment and uncertainty in these early days of true, stepless pyramid construction. The northern one has, by the standards of later pyramids, a rather low angle of incline, but is the first true pyramid of Egypt. Unlike the Djoser monument, these pyramids are notably stark and simple in interior lay-out and quite without decoration inside.

Snofru's chief queen was called Hetepheres and this pair were the parents of the famous Cheops whose Great Pyramid at Giza has always attracted so much interest and speculation. The furniture found by the American team of George Reisner in 1925 at the bottom of the deep shaft near the Great Pyramid in which Hetepheres had been re-buried— almost certainly after the spoliations of tomb-robbers at her original

Dashur grave—is a very impressive indication of the style of life enjoyed by the ruling class of Old Kingdom Egypt. Egypt was at this time a rather self-contained civilization that had rapidly—in a matter of four or five hundred years—elaborated all the very distinctive elements of its culture. It did not possess a foreign empire in the way that it was to come to do a thousand years or so later, but, of course, international relations were taking place. The Palermo Stone records, in the time of Snofru: 'the bringing of forty ships filled with cedar wood', doubtless from Byblos and there is in the Cairo Museum a plaque depicting Snofru smiting bedouin enemies in Sinai, indicated by the hieroglyph for foreign country.

 The sign for 'foreign country'.

Cheops, of around 2600 BC, is personally depicted—as far as material available at present goes—only in the form of one small ivory statuette from Abydos which scarcely does justice to the builder of that mighty monument the Great Pyramid. Tradition, which Herodotus reports, made him the proprietor of this greatest of all pyramids and nineteenth century explorers found his name, in the form of a mason's identification mark, upon one of the blocks in the system of pressure-relieving chambers above the burial room. His remains, of course, were completely missing when modern investigators came to look into his great stone sarcophagus. There is nothing very mysterious about that, since the bodies—and the treasures—of almost every Egyptian king and notable were long since robbed away from their tombs. The ancient Egyptians practised tomb-robbing from the very earliest days: no doubt the development of the royal mastabas of archaic times was partly prompted by the desire to secure the burials from molestation; we have seen that Cheops' mother had had to be moved because of robbers' attentions; Tutankhamun's tomb over a thousand years later was apparently subject to some spoliation within, at the most, a few years of his burial; there exist from New Kingdom times the court records of the trials of Theban tomb-robbers. We cannot be absolutely certain that Cheops was ever buried in his pyramid. There is evidence of earthquake damage inside the pyramid and the very roughly cut vertical passage called a 'robbers' tunnel' may be the route by which workmen, trapped by the accidental release of the plugging blocks during a tremor, made their escape. Such an interpretation remains entirely speculative, but serves to show that nothing should be taken for granted.

Certainly, Cheops would have been mummified for burial. The early stages of the history of mummification are a little obscure, since no true mummies much older than Cheops' time have survived. There are the desert-dessicated predynastic natural mummies, like the one in the British Museum, and no doubt observation of this naturally preservative

Previous page *In a deep shaft at Giza, near the Great Pyramid, was found the burial of Cheops' mother Hetepheres: among her grave-goods was a quantity of fine furniture including a gilded chair, bed and bed-canopy frame. This furniture, expertly conserved and partly reconstructed, is four and a half thousand years old.*

Gold was mined in quantity in Egypt, which was richer in this precious metal than any other country of the ancient Middle East. Gold-working was consequently a well-developed art: this cast gold falcon-head comes from Hieraconpolis and dates to perhaps the Sixth Dynasty, around 2300 BC. About 10 cm high, it was intended to be fitted on a wooden body.

process prompted a more systematic research into embalming techniques. Professor Emery found a sort of pseudo-mummy, with limbs and even digits individually wrapped, in one of his Sakkara Archaic Period excavations, but it does not appear that any of the later processes of mummification had been perpetrated upon it, like removal of the corruptible internal organs for separate treatment or chemical dehydration. One of the oldest true mummies known is that found a few years ago at Sakkara and ascribed to Nefer, a court musician of about the time of Cheops.

The pyramid of Cheops is an awe-inspiring achievement, but that of his near successor Chephren—while seemingly arousing little of the pyramidiotic interest of the lunatic fringe—is very nearly as imposing, being little smaller in overall proportions and indeed appearing from some vantage points a little taller than its predecessor because it stands on higher ground. The third pyramid of Giza, belonging to Chephren's successor Mycerinus, would impress us all in Kew Gardens or Central Park but is dwarfed by its two great neighbours.

The pyramids were not lone monuments standing all by themselves. They were the centre piece of a whole complex of funerary constructions: in the case of the Giza examples, each was surrounded by an enclosure wall and provided on its eastern side with a mortuary temple where the ceremonies of burial and the continuing services of the dead king's cult were carried out; a causeway ran down from this temple towards the river valley where it terminated in another building called the Valley Temple. It was during the Fourth Dynasty that the pre-eminence of the king as a divine ruler identified with the sun-god Re began to be fully expressed: there are foreshadowings of this in earlier dynasties and even a Second Dynasty king carried the name Reneb, 'Re is Lord'; but only in the Fourth Dynasty did this emphasis begin to be played up. The pyramids were a colossal expression of the divine power of the king continuing even in death to brood from the desert's edge over the green valley of the living.

Interestingly, the presumed last king of the Fourth Dynasty, Shepseskaf, deserted pyramid building and went back to a mastaba tomb, the so-called Mastabat Faraun at South Sakkara. Evidently the powers of this dynasty were waning and there is some evidence to suggest that Shepseskaf's own son was not even accorded the title of 'prince' by the founders of the next line.

Fifth Dynasty c2500–2350 BC

During this dynasty, the identification of the king with Re is fully realized: 'Son of Re' is now regularly a part of the titulature of these kings. This period and the earlier part of the next dynasty also marks the artistic zenith of the Old Kingdom style and so, many may think, of Egyptian

Above *The pyramid of Meidum, which has suffered severe collapse, scarcely looks like a pyramid at all.*

Below *The Old Kingdom style of mummification is revealed in the mummy of a Fourth Dynasty official called Nefer.*

The trio of pyramids at Giza, with their smaller satellites, are the best-built of the Egyptian pyramids.

The classic quality of the Old Kingdom art was hardly matched in later days—compare this figure of a Fifth Dynasty noble (above left) with the ugly line and clumsy layout of a Ptolemaic relief from Kom Ombo (above right).

Below From the late Old Kingdom pyramid of king Wenis come these inscriptions recounting magical formulae.

art altogether. The painted reliefs from the famous tomb of Ti at Sakkara well exemplify the purity and economy of style to be found at this time. The contrast with the fussy, distorted and unbalanced style of Ptolemaic times is an easy one to perceive, but even in the best of New Kingdom art it is possible to detect a falling-away from the classical expression of the Old Kingdom.

The tombs of the nobles that lie around the pyramids of the Fourth Dynasty are sparely decorated and cramped in layout, by contrast with the more spacious and elaborated mastabas of the Fifth. It seems clear that the nobles of this time were rising in importance vis-à-vis the king, despite his now fully asserted role as 'Son-of-Re', and were no longer such self-effacing servants as they had been under the Fourth Dynasty rulers. This situation seems to be reflected in the increasingly jerry-built nature of the pyramids erected in the Fifth Dynasty. That of an early Fifth Dynasty king, Userkaf, near the Step Pyramid at Sakkara, already displays recourse to rubble-filled interiors, faced with fine stone, in place of solid construction through and through. This deterioration in building standards is seen at Abusir, between Giza and Sakkara, too: a bold design, which must have looked splendid at the time, is now reduced to tip-like heaps of rubble because roughly piled interiors were merely faced with a cosmetic outer layer of finely finished stone, and once that facing was disturbed the pyramid could only deliquesce into what the novice pyramidologist might not recognize at first sight as a pyramid at all.

For all that, the Fifth Dynasty was a wealthy time, with an increase in foreign trade and involvements. Sahure, who has a pyramid at Abusir, is known to have fought against the Libyans to the north-west and Asiatics to the north-east. Wenis was the last king of this period, and it is in his ruined pyramid at Sakkara that the best-executed of the pyramid texts, with among other things their magical spells about eating gods and men, are found.

Sixth Dynasty 2350–2250 BC

This dynasty is marked by increasing limitations set upon the royal power by the rise of the nobles. Something of the lifestyle and aspirations of some of these nobles is evidenced in the tomb of Mereruka at Sakkara, where a giant statue of the tomb's proprietor strides through his false door to receive offerings brought to him in his house of eternity. Parallel with the rising power of the courtiers of this time ran the recovery of those provincial powers which had waned under the kings' centralized domination since Third or Fourth Dynasty days. Provincial families were on the way to becoming little independent principalities. At Sakkara the badly built and much-decayed pyramids of Teti and Phiops (Piopi, Pepi) I and II seem to bear witness to this circumstance.

It was the pyramid of Phiops I that, in better days, gave Memphis its name. Previously, since Menes' foundation of the city, it had been known as 'The White Wall', or 'White Walls'. Now Phiops I's pyramid complex was called Men-nefer, meaning '(Phiops is) enduring and beautiful' and the Graecized form of this name, as extended to the whole city of the living and the dead, was Memphis. Another of the city's names was Hikuptah, 'Mansion of the soul of Ptah' (Ptah was the patron god of Memphis), and this name, in the Greek form of Aiguptos, was extended to embrace the whole country—'Egypt'.

Phiops II seems to have enjoyed a very long rule indeed, comparable with queen Victoria's, and he is said to have lived for nearly a hundred years. We have a letter he wrote as a child to the leader of an expedition that had been down south in Nubia: 'Come at once to court and bring with you that dwarf, alive and well . . . to gladden the heart of the King of Upper and Lower Egypt.' The 'dwarf' may well have been a pygmy whose ultimate home had lain in the forests of central Africa. Phiops II's long reign seems to have witnessed a growing decline of central authority in favour of the rise of provincial power groups and, after his death, serious internal trouble broke out. There seems to be no question of outside interference in Egyptian affairs: what probably happened was that the burden imposed upon the country as a whole by the royal and priestly centres had become too great to be borne.

Chapter V   Egyptian History in the Ancient World: to the Arab Conquest

First Intermediate Period c2250–2100 BC

At the end of the reign of Phiops II, the social forces already seen at work in the rise of the powers of the courtiers and the provincial families issued in a full-scale collapse of central authority and of the unity of the Egyptian state. At Memphis, the successors of the Sixth Dynasty went on for some time, though they cannot be seen properly to constitute a Seventh Dynasty as per Manetho, who credits the seventy rulers of this unit with reigns of only seventy days apiece! He goes on to allow 146 years to an Eighth Memphis Dynasty, which seems to indicate that Memphite rule persisted with some sort of continuity into this Intermediate Period. Meanwhile at Heracleopolis some way up the Nile, there was a quite independent set of rulers taken together as the Ninth and Tenth Dynasties, who for a time seem to have managed to hold sway over the entire country. Up river still further, at Thebes, another family of provincial nobles was gathering power which eventually overcame the Heracleopolitans and took over the whole of Egypt.

In the other great Near Eastern civilization, that of Mesopotamia, considerable changes had been taking place. Mesopotamian chronology in the third millennium BC is, if anything, even harder to establish than the Egyptian one. But it seems clear that by, say, the time of Cheops in Egypt—that is to say in early dynastic times in Mesopotamia—the Sumerian component in Mesopotamian civilization was waning a little, at least in terms of written language, in the face of the ever-increasing introduction of Semitic-speaking elements. By 2000 BC, a century after the close of Egypt's First Intermediate Period, the old Sumerian language had entirely disappeared as a spoken tongue, becoming a classical heritage for the educated citizens of Mesopotamia, and been replaced by a Semitic language (albeit one influenced by much borrowing from Sumerian). The Akkadians, who took power under Sargon in about 2370 BC, are the first named Semitic group in Mesopotamia: their rule began during Egypt's Sixth Dynasty, perhaps a decade or so before Phiops II came to the Egyptian throne. The Third Dynasty of Ur, a sort of Sumerian Renaissance in Lower Mesopotamia, roughly co-incides with the ending of the First Intermediate Period in Egypt by the Theban princes.

Byblos in Lebanon was important to the Egyptians from the Archaic Period onwards and it is interesting to note that this was already a city of some age when the Egyptians first became involved with it. It seems to have been an ultimately Sumerian inspiration that formed the character of Byblos before Egyptian influences were felt. The city—which was later the centre of the Semitic-speaking Phoenicians' commercial activities— may well have been the trading centre through which Egyptians acquired the semi-precious stone lapis lazuli that we know to have originated in the first place in Afghanistan (one can imagine the chain of barter that brought it to Lebanon!) and which occurs in Egyptian contexts from early dynastic times. The Byblos traders were presumably the agents who took Egyptian goods, like stone vessels and furniture, around the ancient world—some furniture of the Fifth Dynasty has been discovered in a grave in north-west Turkey. The Egyptians knew Byblos by the name of 'Kpn' and called all ocean-going boats 'Kebenwet', Byblos-boats. A good deal of Egyptian material from the Sixth Dynasty has been found at Byblos, but after that time (and after some sort of destruction had been carried out at Byblos by nomadic intruders) no more Egyptian remains occur for some time and evidently trade had ceased. The Egyptians themselves had, in any case, fallen upon hard times at the end of the Sixth Dynasty as we have seen.

By contrast with the peaceful trade dealings Egypt enjoyed with Byblos, Egyptian involvement in Sinai and Palestine was simply exploitative. The Egyptians were certainly after turquoise in this region (remember the bracelets on the arm from the Archaic Period royal 'tomb' at Abydos) and, though they had other sources, they may well have been interested in copper mining too. In the Sixth Dynasty, violent clashes with the inhabitants of Palestine and Syria are recorded in some Egyptian tomb reliefs and there is little doubt that the Egyptians were plundering cattle and carrying off some slaves from these western Asian townships during the years preceding the First Intermediate Period.

Middle Kingdom c2100–1700 BC *Eleventh Dynasty 2100–2000* BC

Three of the Theban kings whose growing power had overthrown the Heracleopolitan rulers of the Ninth and Tenth Dynasties were called Mentuhotep. The first of these, Mentuhotep Nebhepetre, is known for his mortuary temple at Deir el-Bahri, opposite Luxor on the West Bank at Thebes, which reverted to a mastaba form rather like the proto-

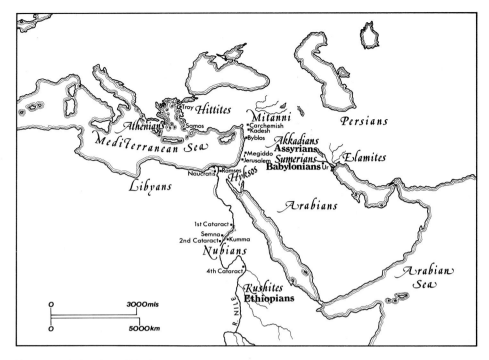

Egypt and the river Nile in the Ancient World.

pyramids of the Archaic Period. Its terraced structure served as a pattern for the later and spectacular mortuary temple of queen Hatshepsut alongside it. In fact Mentuhotep's monument well reflects his status as a provincial ruler on his way to becoming king of Egypt: partly a rock-cut tomb on the provincial pattern but with intimations of the old royal pyramid style. Under the unified rule of his dynasty, Egyptian trade picked up again and voyages down the Red Sea to somewhere on the East African coast, at a point called Pwenet or Punt by the ancient Egyptians, are recorded from this period.

Twelfth Dynasty 2000–1800 BC

This was a prosperous time for ancient Egypt, with many determined and powerful rulers who dealt, in no uncertain terms, with Egypt's neighbours to the north and south. A good deal of building up and down the land was undertaken by these kings.

A complete return to the royal tradition of pyramid-burial occurred, though the pyramids were rather in the tradition of the shoddier Fifth and Sixth Dynasty constructions than the well-built examples of Snofru,

97

Cheops and Chephren. To Ammenemes I belongs the north pyramid at Lisht, well south of Cairo, who seems to have lost his life in a classic harem conspiracy. He left to his son an account of one unsuccessful attempt along these lines when his enemies had got at him through his own household: 'The men who came against me were the men whom I had trusted and made rich. They had sworn great oaths that their loyalty would last while life endured'.

Sesostris I (Senusret, Senwosnet) of about 1950 BC was a powerful military commander who pacified Nubia to the south of Egypt—his is the south pyramid at Lisht. Sesostris II built his pyramid at El-Lahun: among the ruins of the houses in which his builders lived while working on his tomb there was found some quantity of Cretan pottery, while in Crete itself Egyptian objects of this period have been unearthed. Sesostris III of about 1860 BC consolidated Egyptian power in Nubia, building the fortresses of Semna and Kumma above the Second Cataract to control Nubian immigration into Egypt. He also conducted campaigns against the 'miserable Asiatics' (in Sinai the Egyptians were certainly mining copper by this time) and his several portrait-statues reveal a very stern-faced personality, every inch the warrior we know him to have been. His pyramid is at Dashur.

Ammenemes III greatly developed the Fayum region, that depression to the west of the Nile above Cairo that was fed by a branch of the Nile and was largely taken up by a fluctuating lake. Dams and canals with sluices were installed to control the Nile's feeding of the Fayum (and so as to use the Fayum lake as a reservoir of river water) and an area of the lake-bed was reclaimed for rich agricultural land. At the entrance to the Fayum Ammenemes III built his pyramid at Hawara and alongside it an unusually complex and many-roomed mortuary temple which later Greek travellers identified as Daedalus' Labyrinth. Herodotus was very taken with it: '. . . the Labyrinth surpasses even the pyramids'. Today nothing remains but a field of low and unprepossessing mounds around the pyramid.

At the end of this dynasty there is reason to think that a queen named Sebek-nofru ruled with pharaonic powers.

Thirteenth Dynasty 1800–1700 BC

Over this century, when there were a lot of rulers (frequently named Sebek-hotep), royal power gradually dwindled as it had done at the end of the Sixth Dynasty but this time things became so serious that in the Second Intermediate Period of collapse non-Egyptian rulers were able to take power in Lower Egypt and even subject the princes of Upper Egypt to some sort of vassalage.

Second Intermediate Period c*1700–1550* BC

These foreign rulers, the Hyksos, are sometimes called 'the Shepherd Kings', after a misapprehension of Manetho's as to what Hyksos might mean. It probably means simply 'foreign chiefs'. They came from somewhere to the east of the Delta, which was the initial scene of their rule in Egypt. Asiatics had been coming into the country in the service of the Thirteenth Dynasty well before the arrival of the Hyksos rulers. The situation somewhat resembles the last days of the Roman Empire when foreign mercenaries from eastern Europe were taken on by the last emperors to deal with the troubles they already had, bringing many more problems in their wake.

The Hyksos stronghold in the Delta was Avaris. The Hyksos must have been in the main a collection of western Asiatics who entered the eastern Delta at this time in rapidly increasing numbers possibly as the result of displacement from their homelands either directly at the hands of Indo-European ingressors or of other (semitic) groups whom the Indo-Europeans had already displaced. This is the time, in the first few centuries of the second millennium BC when the first Indo-European-speaking groups were coming down from somewhere behind the Caucasus into the Greek mainland (and then the islands) and into western Asia, where they appear in the historical record as the Hittites and the kingdom of Mitanni. It is only fair to say that speculations about the invasion of Indo-European speakers are based more upon language considerations (the occurrence at this time of Indo-European names in Akkadian documents) than upon hard archaeological evidence of the irruption of new peoples. Nevertheless it is tempting to relate the arrival of the Hyksos with a general Indo-European 'Volk-wanderung' of the early centuries of the second millennium BC.

The Hyksos were not in all probability very foreign to the Egyptians who knew them already as close neighbours to the east of the Delta or even as mercenary forces within Egypt. It seems equally true to say that Egyptian ways were not at all foreign to the Hyksos who seem to have rapidly gone over to Egyptian customs once they began to settle and hold sway in the Delta. Manetho assigned to them the Fifteenth and Sixteenth Dynasties. (The Fourteenth was a short-lived native Egyptian Dynasty 'ruling' in the Delta while the Thirteenth was still in force in Upper Egypt.) But in reality the 'Lesser Hyksos' of the Sixteenth Dynasty seem only to have been petty chiefs under the shadow of their powerful contemporaries, the 'Greater Hyksos' of the Fifteenth Dynasty. A few of the names of these kings will suffice to show that, although they rapidly went over to Egyptian ways (as most intrusive rulers of Egypt did in later times), they were of exotic origin: Yakub-Her; Staan; Khyan. The last of their line with any claim to rule the whole of Egypt was called Apophis, an Egyptian name.

The Hyksos left little behind them in the way of monuments, and no statue or relief portrays a single Hyksos ruler. They did introduce into Egypt the extensive use of the horse for purposes of warfare. The horse may just have been known in Egypt before their coming, but it was thanks to the Hyksos that any great use was made of it thereafter and that the charioteering form of combat was adopted by the Egyptians of the New Kingdom. The wheel itself was little employed by the Egyptians, until after the Hyksos rule. Although the potter's wheel was known and the wheel principle was applied to shaping wood and stone, for purposes of land-transport sledges and rollers were preferred until New Kingdom times. Less tangibly, the Hyksos brought to Egypt an involvement in western Asiatic affairs that went beyond warfare into realms of social outlook and philosophy that all the innate conservatism of ancient Egypt could not shake off again. The old divine kings of an Egypt sufficient unto itself became, in the New Kingdom, warrior-heroes after the pattern familiar from Homer, deeply involved in a diplomatic and imperial entanglement with the powers of western Asia.

Seventeenth Dynasty 1600–1550 BC

It was the princes of Thebes who first shook off the Hyksos yoke and then expelled them from Egypt altogether. The mummy of one of the first rulers of the Seventeenth Dynasty was found in a royal cache hidden high up in the cliff at Deir el-Bahri opposite Luxor. This mummy, of king Sekenenre III, is extensively mutilated with knife wounds and axe blows and it is tempting to see in these injuries the results of his campaigning against the Hyksos; but perhaps he was assassinated in a palace revolution on his own side. Sekenenre's queen was called Aahotep and she is credited with having rallied the Theban forces against the Hyksos. Her mummy was found in a tomb near the entrance of the Valley of the Kings on the West Bank at Thebes and it, and the jewellery found with it, are now in the Cairo Museum. The jewels include a very striking collection of military honours, awarded for her valiant part in the expulsion of the Hyksos, such as daggers and (oddly, to our eyes) great gold flies. Aahotep's son, Kemose, pursued the war against the Hyksos but it was his brother Amosis who finally reunited Egypt and reigned through the founding years of the New Kingdom from about 1575 to 1550 BC. Amun was, at least from the beginning of Middle Kingdom times, the chief god of the Thebans, a hidden god associated with the wind. With the rise of Theban power, Amun became the dominant divinity of the New Kingdom, identified as Amun-Re with the older sun-god of the earlier dynasties.

New Kingdom 1550–712 BC *Eighteenth Dynasty 1550–1350* BC

This dynasty numbers among its rulers some of the most famous and infamous pharaohs of Egypt. 'Pharaoh' becomes during this period a legitimate designation of the kings of ancient Egypt: we have it through the Bible, where an Egyptian original something like *per-ao* was rendered in the form we know, strictly meaning 'great house' but at this time applied to the government of Egypt and its head.

The second king of the dynasty, Tuthmosis I, is the first of the long line of pharaohs buried in rock-cut tombs in the Valley of the Kings: for Egyptian royalty at least, the pyramid was an obsolete monument. He was a considerable warrior, campaigning in the south and into Asia, raiding as far as the Euphrates river on one occasion. But in the last years of his reign (he died about 1500 BC) his children fought over the succession and may have ruled together at certain periods. Tuthmosis II probably did not survive for many years and his remarkable sister Hatshepsut appears to have ruled as a pharaoh in her own right between about 1495 and 1470 BC. Her outstanding monument is her great mortuary temple at Deir el-Bahri across the Nile from Luxor. This three-terraced temple is an impressive landmark set in a sort of natural bay in the high red cliffs of the Theban Hills. The reliefs on its walls, which sometimes show Hatshepsut in all the formal accoutrements of pharaoh (she is seen in male dress, and sporting the ceremonial false-beard of kingship), include a long series depicting the divine birth that was supposed to be a pre-condition of rule. The religious view was that the rulers of Egypt were fathered by the sun-god himself on the chief queen of the preceding king, the so-called 'Great First Wife', without of course denying the paternity of the real father at the same time.

Another series at Deir el-Bahri recounts the adventures of an expedition to Punt during Hatshepsut's reign, to obtain gold, ivory, incense, trees and animals in return for Egyptian manufactures. The narrative is enlivened by the appearance of the chieftainess of Punt as an extremely obese lady indeed. And yet another panel records the bringing down by boat from the quarries at Aswan of two huge obelisks for erection in the Karnak temple: one of them still stands there and is interesting because it has come down a little askew on its base and remained so for three and a half thousand years.

When Hatshepsut died, and was perhaps buried in the tomb she had prepared for herself in the Valley of the Kings, her younger brother came into sole possession of the Egyptian throne as Tuthmosis III. However much he may have been overshadowed by his sister during her rule, Tuthmosis III soon established himself as one of the most powerful and significant of the kings of ancient Egypt. He ruled from about 1500 to 1440 BC, but his real power dated from Hatshepsut's death in about 1470 BC. He really put Egypt on the map in western Asia, conquering Palestine

Left *On the West Bank at Thebes, set in a natural bay of the cliffs, stands the three-terraced mortuary temple of Hatshepsut, a ruling queen of the New Kingdom.*

Below left *Among the reliefs carved in Hatshepsut's temple is a picture of the obese queen of Punt, a land somewhere down the east African coast where the Egyptians traded.*

Below *Among the powerful warrior kings of the Middle Kingdom reigned the stern-faced Sesostris III.*

and Syria with the bold siege of Megiddo. His enemies seem to have been a loose alliance of petty princelings organized by the prince of Kadesh (on the river Orontes) to frustrate Egyptian trade and influence in this vitally important commercial area. Perhaps memories of the Hyksos influx of two or three generations before helped with the Egyptians' determination to deal with their western neighbours; perhaps it was simply the need to secure Egyptian commercial interests among them. But what Tuthmosis III did went far beyond the temporary raiding his predecessors had sometimes carried out to the east of the Delta. He consciously set about the establishment of a permanent imperial hold upon western Asia. The princelings of Palestine and Syria were formally to become client-rulers on behalf of an Egypt recognized by all to hold sway over the region. Regular shows of force by the Egyptian army were to be a feature of empire here, and fighting was sometimes required. Kadesh itself was twice subdued and Tuthmosis III also fought against the (predominantly) Indo-European Kingdom of Mitanni on the Upper Euphrates, which had similar and conflicting imperial designs on western Asia. Throughout the area, small Egyptian garrisons were planted and Egyptian commissioners took up residence to handle Egyptian interests and keep an eye on the client-princes.

All these unaccustomed innovations were bound to bring great domestic changes upon Egypt itself: on a material level, great wealth came into Egypt from the imperial holdings; a standing army on a much more regular footing than hitherto was made necessary by the military demands of empire; new classes of commercial administrators and diplomats were called into being and the old order of Egyptian society was upset; for the first time, a trading class was allowed to operate with some independence of the Egyptian government. Psychological changes, too, were the order of the day: the old insularity and self-sufficiency of Egypt were rendered untenable by the new developments; cosmopolitan ideas (and the princes of western Asia seem to have been very cosmopolitan men) strayed into the Egyptian consciousness; the role of the pharaoh was altered in a way that required of him much more demonstration of his capacity for military and diplomatic success in place of mere reliance on his divine standing. The 'Amarna tablets' which belong to this Eighteenth Dynasty, are the remains of an international correspondence between some of the rulers of the time. Not even the Egyptian language was employed in international diplomacy among the great powers and their client states, rather it was Akkadian cuneiform (writing, in a Semitic language, on clay tablets by means of wedge-like signs).

Amenophis III, Tuthmosis III's successor by three is the pharaoh to whom the earlier part of the Amarna correspondence relates. In accordance with the wealth and imperial posture of his kingdom, he built on a considerable scale (so did Tuthmosis III). The 'Colossi of Memnon' (as the Greeks dubbed them) are two great statues that once stood in front of a now all-but-vanished temple of his. With Amenophis III we enter upon that vivid, unusually well-illuminated and all-too-human cycle of events to which belong the beautiful queen Nefertiti, the deformed heretic Akhenaten and Tutankhamun of the household name.

When Amenophis III died, in perhaps 1367 BC and apparently after some years of ill-health (his mummy, if it really is his, points to a poor physical condition, and tooth-ache must have plagued him), he was succeeded by his son, called at first Amenophis IV. To judge by the majority of the depictions of this king, he was something of a physical monster— with an elongated face, epicene breasts and thighs and a bulging belly, the whole unmistakably indicating some gross glandular upset. Retrospective diagnosis of historical figures (especially where, as in this case, their physical remains are missing) is a risky business, but two glandular conditions known as Fröhlich's and the Eunuchoidal Syndrome have been proposed by way of explaining his appearance. That great beauty Nefertiti (to judge by her famous bust, now in Berlin, and the even more affecting unfinished study in the Cairo Museum) was his queen. Her origins, whether as foreigner or half-sister of Amenophis IV or Egyptian commoner, remain a matter only for speculation.

It is possible that Amenophis III, during his illnesses, allowed his imperial responsibilities to slide a little and likely that Amenophis IV let them go a lot further. There are, among the Amarna letters, some rather desperately repeated appeals for his help from clients in Palestine; either he would not or could not meet these appeals. What is certain is that Amenophis IV was much concerned with something of more domestic significance for Egypt. Already in his father's time, a shift in religious emphasis is detectable towards the cult of the sun-god Re (now identified with Amun) in a very particular aspect, that of the physical disk of the sun called the 'Aten'. In his early years of rule, Amenophis IV seems to have been content with the divine organization he found in being at his accession: early reliefs show him offering to Amun. After a time, he came to nurse a colossal antipathy towards Amun in particular, and all the old gods in general, save for the Aten disk. Whether this was motivated by a real hatred for Amun and company as ideological entities or by some wish or need to go against the established (and rich and powerful!) priesthood of Amun at Thebes is another matter for speculation. It is doubtful whether Amenophis IV was any more capable than Oliver Cromwell of strictly distinguishing between social forces and their ideological expressions. It is pointless to guess at the effect his presumed glandular disabilities may have had on these affairs.

Akhenaten took some drastic courses of action as a result of his convictions: he instituted a widespread and thorough assault upon the old gods (erasing their names wherever they occurred, even high up on

Bas-relief carvings in Egyptian tombs were frequently vividly painted: these noble ladies, smelling flowers, come from a Middle Kingdom tomb. They wear the sheer white dresses of the female nobility and 'pectorals' around their necks.

The surpassing piece of
ancient Egyptian gold-work
that has come down to us is
the solid inner coffin of
Tutankhamun, of beaten
22-carat gold. If this minor
and unregarded pharaoh was
sent to his grave in such lavish
style, then the treasures of
the great kings can only be
dimly imagined.

temple walls or on seemingly insignificant little objects) and shifting his capital right away from the Thebes of his ancestors to a virgin site down river called by him 'the Horizon of the Aten' and known today as Amarna. He changed his name, to incorporate his beloved Aten, into Akhenaten, which may mean something like 'It goes well with the Aten'. We may well guess at the response all this elicited in the hearts of the Amun priesthood but we do not know what effect it had upon the Egyptian people as a whole. It is hard to believe that their religious conservatism can have found much place for this kind of sweeping change. In any case, Akhenaten does not seem to have looked upon his Aten-cult as suitable for mass consumption—it was restricted very much to his own family and a few courtiers, while the people of Egypt were expected to go on approaching their pharaoh as a living manifestation of deity in a manner that harked back to Old Kingdom attitudes. There is no denying a sometimes moving quality to Akhenaten's 'Hymn to the Sun' and his emphasis upon that Egyptian concept (sometimes personified, even by the 'monotheistic' Akhenaten, as a goddess) 'Maat', which is difficult to translate and means something like 'righteousness, justice, truth'; but most of the pictures of Akhenaten that have been painted by his admirers are hopelessly speculative and given to suppressing the less attractive aspect of his religious revolution.

More or less coincident with the reign of Akhenaten, and probably owing much to the emphasis he put upon 'Maat-truthfulness', is the art-style called the 'Amarna style', but not of course restricted to the site of Amarna only. One is tempted to call it an un-Egyptian style, for it so largely forsakes that reliance upon convention and prescribed forms which Egyptian art as a whole displays. In keeping with Akhenaten's interpretation of 'Maat', a more naturalistic expression comes over the artistic products of this time: the heads of Nefertiti and of queen Tiy exhibit these new qualities, as do the wall paintings from Amarna in the Cairo Museum.

The troubled times of Akhenaten and his immediate successors have been a great field for practical archaeology. Excavations at Amarna before the First World War and between the wars were a revelation of the art and everyday life of these times. The bust of Nefertiti came from a sculptor's workshop and was carried off to Germany so easily because in its uncleaned state little hint of its splendours was given away. In the 1970s interest has focused upon Akhenaten's pre-Amarna days, in the form of the Aten temples he built at Karnak which were purposely demolished by a close successor: thousands of blocks from these temples, many of them carrying, like jigsaw-pieces, fragments of the design which they went to make up, are being patiently sorted and photographically matched-up in an attempt to reconstruct the reliefs themselves and the temple they decorated. The poor little tombs of Akhenaten's two immediate successors (who were perhaps his half-brothers) were excavated in the earlier quarter of this century, one of them (uniquely full of riches, being that rarest of things a nearly unplundered ancient Egyptian tomb) belonged to the short-lived king Tutankhaten, who changed his name, in a return to the old religious orthodoxy, to Tutankhamun. The other, a makeshift and disturbed burial, contained a body that has recently been shown to be very closely related by blood to Tutankhamun's mummy and may be that of a brother, Smenkhkare, who perhaps ruled jointly with Akhenaten for a short while. Akhenaten's own empty tomb is known but of the physical remains of 'that Criminal of Amarna' (as he was known to his orthodox Egyptian successors) and of Nefertiti not a trace has survived.

The last three decades of the fourteenth century BC were ruled over in Egypt by a former generalissimo of Akhenaten's and Tutankhamun's named Horemheb. He is the last king of the Eighteenth Dynasty, and later generations were inclined to regard him as the first legitimate monarch since Amenophis III. Tutankhamun's widow had tried to carry on as queen of Egypt by writing to the king of the Hittites in Anatolia to ask him to send her a son whom she would marry and so make pharaoh. He never arrived, and Ankhesenamun married a court official named Ay who ruled for four years before Horemheb. Horemheb seems to have put most of his energies not into foreign relations but into setting his Egyptian house in order. He fully revived the cults of the old gods and re-endowed their priesthoods with land and cattle; and he demolished what was left of Akhenaten's memorials; he is responsible for mutilating and using as rubble many of the carved blocks from Akhenaten's Theban temple.

Nineteenth Dynasty c *1300–1200* BC

A new family, of Delta origins, came to power with this dynasty, and during this time engagements in western Asia came back to the fore, while some new enemies materialized in the Mediterranean.

Sethos I (Seti I), to whom belongs a very impressive tomb in the Valley of the Kings which completely dwarfs, as do several others, the tiny but more famous tomb of Tutankhamun, was a great fighter in western Asia. He especially had to contend with the Hittite kingdom which was now seriously threatening Egyptian interests in Palestine and Syria. His son was the inevitable Ramesses II, ruling from about 1290 to 1225 BC who left his unmistakable mark all over Egypt. He was a grandiose builder in his own right (the great Hypostyle Hall at Karnak and the temple of Abu Simbel are owed to him) and even where he did not build he often superimposed his name upon existing monuments, usually cut indelibly deep and so easily recognizable. He lived to a very great age and is supposed to have fathered multitudes of children; his mummy is one of the best preserved in the Cairo Museum. He fought the Hittites on and off for

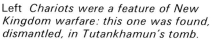

Left *Chariots were a feature of New Kingdom warfare: this one was found, dismantled, in Tutankhamun's tomb.*

Below *Akhenaten's statues frequently show him as a grotesquely deformed figure but, towards the end of his reign, the excesses of the 'Amarna' style seem to have been toned down.*

Below *The mother of Akhenaten, queen Tiy, is powerfully portrayed in this small wooden head.*

Next page *Nefertiti was the beautiful queen of the heretic Akhenaten: she may have enjoyed a virtually equal authority with him.*

over twenty years, with a great battle at Kadesh on the Orontes that he celebrated in a gigantic relief on one of the walls of his mortuary temple on the West Bank at Thebes and upon other of his constructions. (His, by the way, is the fallen statue supposed to have inspired Shelley's poem about Ozymandias, King of Kings.) Finally Ramesses II made peace with the Hittites and the treaty is carved in hieroglyphs on a wall in the Karnak temple. The treaty gives northern Syria to the Hittites and Palestine to the Egyptians and expresses a fulsome regard for each other on the part of the two powers. Ramesses II married a Hittite princess.

When eventually Ramesses II died, only one son in the line of succession survived his long reign, Menephthes (Merneptah) who carried on fighting the Libyans in the north-west, as well as meeting the first sallies of a federation of states attacking from the Mediterranean Sea, among them Indo-European speakers from the Mediterranean islands. After him came three short reigns and a period of decline.

The story of the Israelites in Egypt and their exodus under Moses might belong to roughly this time. Moses' presumed ancestors would have been living under Egyptian rule since the time of Tuthmosis III and perhaps since the Hyksos, with perhaps a period of greater autonomy during the Amarna episode. With the restoration of empire under the Nineteenth Dynasty, the bedouins of Sinai and the Semitic-speakers of Palestine were brought back under Egyptian charge and some of them were conscripted to work on pharaonic projects in Egypt, notably in the eastern Delta where the old Hyksos capital Avaris had become a Nineteenth Dynasty stronghold. The Biblical cities of Pithom and Ramses were situated here. The story of the escape of the Israelites possibly reflects an opportunity seized to get out of Egypt while the going was good in the latter days of the Nineteenth Dynasty.

Twentieth Dynasty c 1200–1100 BC

At the beginning of this dynasty, Ramesses III had to face the Libyans and the 'Sea Peoples' again. Troy was being sacked at about this time on the coast of Asia Minor and the Greek mainlanders were becoming a force in the Mediterranean. In Egypt, the priesthood of Amun—more than recovered from Akhenaten's attentions—was growing greatly in power. Ramesses III built his very attractive mortuary temple at Medinet Habu across the river from Luxor and is thought to have died as the result of a harem conspiracy, living long enough to initiate the prosecution of his assailants and prescribe their suicides.

Through the reigns of Ramesses IV to Ramesses XII, the Amun priesthood increased its power and wealth and the very throne of Egypt was for a time occupied by the high priest Herihor.

Twenty-first Dynasty 1100–950 BC

This dynasty arose in Tanis of the Delta in response to the collapse of the Theban Ramessides. The high priest Herihor had no pretence to rule all of Egypt, for the Tanis princes were already a law unto themselves in the Delta. A sort of shared rule between the Upper Egyptian high priests and the Delta princes now ensued. About this time a certain Wenamun set off from Thebes to fetch wood from Byblos to build a ceremonial boat for Amun. The surviving story of his adventures takes him to the Delta court and thence to Byblos where a vivid demonstration of the decline of Egypt's prestige and the new independence of her former clients is afforded by the off-hand treatment Wenamun receives at the hands of the local prince.

By this time Nubia was free of Egypt and Palestine lost. In the Amarna letters client rulers had styled themselves to the pharaohs as 'your servant and the dust upon which you tread'. Says the Prince of Byblos to Wenamun: 'I am not the servant of him who sent you'. The prince even employs on his Egyptian guest a board-room technique of modern times, conducting the interview with his back to a sunlit window.

An arresting sidelight on the decline of Egyptian self-confidence at home is shed at about this time by changes in the character of what was depicted in the tombs of the dead. Egyptian culture is known to us, largely, from mortuary remains. This has inclined the casual investigator of ancient Egypt to come away with a morbid impression of the whole civilization. For most of Egyptian history nothing could be further from the truth: the tombs are full of lively scenes of everyday life in the fields or gardens or at parties—that is, until the time of the Nineteenth and Twentieth Dynasties, when the morbid aspects of death and judgement in the underworld are greatly emphasized and tricked out with a much enlarged apparatus of spells and magical devices.

Twenty-second Dynasty 950–750 BC

The Libyans whom the Ramessides had been obliged to fight, had subsequently been serving in Egypt as mercenary troops. They now took advantage of the decline of the native Egyptian powers to found a dynasty of their own. Sheshonk (the Shishak of the Bible) overcame the last of the Tanite princes and went on to campaign with some success against Egypt's western Asiatic enemies. He even took the city of Jerusalem for a time and sacked the temple of Solomon in about 930 BC. After him, another decline into fragmented principalities occurred and, in Upper Egypt, the kings of Kush to the south won power.

Twenty-third and Twenty-fourth Dynasties 750–712 BC

Doomed attempts were made by a succession of various Lower Egyptian princes to carve out some independence for themselves, but they were defeated by the Kushites in control of Upper Egypt.

Late Period 712–332 BC   *Twenty-fifth Dynasty 712–663* BC

This was a dynasty of Ethiopians from the Kushite kingdom, with their capital as far south as the Fourth Cataract. The Nubian part of their domains had been free of Egyptian rule since the latter Ramessides and their control of Upper Egypt itself dated from the Twenty-third Dynasty. Though their homeland lay so far to the south, their culture was vastly imitative of Egypt's and indeed they were more Egyptian than the Egyptians in many ways, especially in religious matters where they were fiercely conservative. A tendency to resurrect the forms and styles of Egypt in its bygone days of glory can be detected in the monuments of the Ethiopian dynasties. They attempted to interfere in western Asiatic affairs, assisting Syria and Palestine against the Assyrians who were now firmly in control in northern Mesopotamia, while the Babylonians ruled the southern Mesopotamian region. After 670 BC, when the Ethiopian Taharka (Tirhakah of the Bible) was beaten by the Assyrians, Egypt itself fell into Assyrian hands, where it substantially remained until a native Egyptian dynasty from the Delta town of Saïs was able to throw out both the Assyrians (distracted by struggles at home and with Elam to their east) and the Ethiopians and bring the native Egyptian principalities back under central rule. This was in about 663 BC.

Twenty-sixth Dynasty 663–525 BC

The Saïte Dynasty, so-called after the hometown Saïs of these rulers, became at this late hour a new age of Egyptian prosperity. Trade flourished, especially with the Greeks who were now laying the foundations of their own classical age. The Saïtes may have been prosperous, but they were backward-looking. They not only restored the fading monuments of their Egyptian past (as when they shored up the roof of the burial chamber in Djoser's Third Dynasty pyramid, now over two thousand years old); they went further and consciously imitated the past, in art and in literature and in the resurrection of old official titles and so on. The whole air is rather reminiscent of the Gothic revival of Victorian times. Psammetichus was the founder of the Saïte Dynasty, and his immediate successor Necho felt confident enough to invade Syria once more while the Assyrians were again distracted. At another engagement at Megiddo, Necho vanquished the Judean king Josiah, but was himself defeated by Nebuchadnezzar of Babylon at Carchemish on the Euphrates, so losing what had been regained in Syria and Palestine. Necho is remarkable for having started work on a canal to link the Nile with the Red Sea, extending an existing channel that ran from the eastern Delta town of Bubastis to lake Timsah. From about 589 to 570 BC, king Apries (to give him one of his Greek names—the Egyptians called him something like Weh-eb-re and the Bible knows him as Hophrah) tried to get back the Syrian possessions until his failure caused a military revolt and a general was put upon the throne. Amasis abandoned designs on western Asia when Nebuchadnezzar threatened Egypt itself. Significantly, Amasis consigned the town of Naucratis close by the Mediterranean to Greek traders who turned it into the country's most important commercial centre. This was the beginning of direct Greek involvement in Egyptian affairs. Amasis also made an alliance with Polycrates, the tyrant of the Greek island of Samos.

The Last Dynasties 525–323 BC and the end of Ancient Egypt

The Twenty-seventh Dynasty was entirely made up of Persian rulers, for Egypt fell into the hands of the expanding Persian Empire under Cambyses, which was simultaneously coming into conflict with the Greek city-states. During this period the canal from the Nile to the Red Sea was completed and Herodotus visited Egypt. The Persians had to contend with a revolt in which the Egyptians were aided by the Athenians and eventually the native Egyptians regained power in the form of the short-lived Twenty-eighth to Thirtieth Dynasties. Among the kings of the Thirtieth Dynasty, Nectanebo I was a strong ruler for his day, and a considerable builder at Philae and Medinet Habu and at Karnak where he erected a pylon-gate.

After 341 BC, Egypt fell back under Persian sway until the conquest of Alexander the Great. He and the Ptolemaic rulers who came after him (so-called after Alexander's general Ptolemy to whom went Egypt after the conqueror's death) ruled as Greeks but with due respect to the native customs of the country, putting themselves forward as very pharaohs in the long line of ancient Egyptian succession. Alexandria was founded by Alexander himself, and he is supposed to have been buried there. Under the Ptolemys a great deal of building was done all over Egypt and some of the best preserved of Egyptian temples belong substantially to this period, like Edfu and Philae. Magnificent as they are, a strain of confusion and decadence is all too apparent in the decoration of these late temples: one has only to compare the classical economy and purity of the Old Kingdom reliefs with the fussy, overloaded and downright ugly carvings of the Ptolemaic monuments.

Under the Ptolemys, the country's fortunes ebbed and flowed for three centuries and a Greek cast was permanently put upon the latter-day civilization of ancient Egypt. Interpenetration of ideas between the

Egyptian and the Greek cultures was very extensive and, indeed, the traditions and mythologies of the whole of the ancient world were mingled here. This was the circumstance in which the philosophical and religious ideas of three or four millennia of Middle Eastern civilization were summarized into new forms at about the time of Christ.

After 200 BC, the mounting power of a hill-top city in Italy began to make itself felt all over the Mediterranean. Rome's involvement in Egypt was at first diplomatic, but after 30 BC Egypt became a Roman province, and after Augustus the Roman emperors styled themselves in their turn as successors of the pharaohs. Another blend of civilizations was achieved in Egypt and Egyptian gods were imported to Rome, in particular the mother goddess Isis and the resurrection-god Osiris-Apis. In the early centuries AD both Alexandrian scepticism and early Christianity flourished in Egypt. The Christians were sometimes persecuted by the Roman authorities, but some may think that they more than got their own back in their pious destruction of the ancient monuments and in the perpetration of such outrages as the stoning of the philosopher Hypatia in AD 415.

In AD 641 the country fell to its latest invaders (until the Turks, the French and the British) with the Islamic conquest of the Arabs, now powerfully radiating out from their homeland in the Arabian peninsula and armed with a vigorous warrior-religion. Islam became the predominant belief of the country (though many 'Coptic' Christians survived) and Arabic the universal language. Save as folklore—like the tales of Aladdin's treasure cave—or in the form of local cults of the saints—like Abu Haggag of Luxor who is paraded on his feast-day in a boat as once was Amun of Thebes—the culture of ancient Egypt, if not her colossal monuments, was lost to view.

Chapter VI Ancient Egyptian Society

The survey of ancient Egyptian history has revealed that major social changes did occur in the course of this civilization's development and decline. There were periods of social collapse, when central rule vanished; there were foreign invasions and, during the New Kingdom, strong foreign influences which brought about altered styles of life; there was an ideological 'democratization' throughout Egyptian history which spread attitudes, for example towards the next life, down from the king or nobility to all classes of society; there was a considerable change in the precise status of the king who went from very god in Old Kingdom times to much more of a warrior chief in the New Kingdom. But there was no revolution in the course of Egyptian history, no 'republicanism', and no blue-prints were ever advanced for a completely reformed social structure. The selective 'anti-clericalism' of Akhenaten came from the top and involved no re-organization of social or economic classes. Nothing to compare with the conflicts of the Patrician and Popular parties in ancient Rome or the rise of the urban proletariat and the development of the great estates of the Roman Empire ever occurred in ancient Egypt. From Menes to the Ptolemys stretches a line of kings and pharaohs without Lord Protectors or Levellers or Popular Assemblies, and always backed up by a group of nobles, provincial governors, priests and scribes. No kings were ever expelled like Tarquin or the tyrants of the Greek city-states (though some fell to conspiracies), and no democracies of however limited a sort ever flourished in Egypt.

Egypt even so was not an oriental despotism of the sort of the Ottoman Empire or a totalitarian state in the manner of modern examples. As with matters of Egyptian religious belief, an imaginative leap is necessary into a social situation not paralleled in recent experience in order to understand this ancient society.

The central role of pharaoh is undoubtedly the essential feature of ancient Egyptian society. In theory, everything belonged to the king, the whole land of Egypt, all its goods and products, all its people. It is interesting to note here that throughout Egyptian history from the very earliest dynastic days, the king always owned sole rights to quarry stone up and down the land or send expeditions for it into desert regions; one of the principal ways in which loyal service could be rewarded was with the grant of fine stone for the servant's tomb. Of course, in reality much ownership of land was in the hands of rich nobles or priestly foundations. Even so, pharaoh remained a very big landowner with private domains all over the country. Sometimes the king was able to take over lands where the funerary bequests of former owners (which were meant to pay for their upkeep) had fallen into abeyance. On the other hand, royal lands were themselves sometimes taken over by independent owners: re-distributions occurred, particularly after times of social trouble, like the Intermediate Periods, or after famines and starvations. After the end of the Old Kingdom, temple lands were continually extended, with much ownership in the hands of the various priesthoods, particularly as time went by of the priesthood of Amun. These lands were exempt from taxes and their personnel were free of military duties in a way that resembles the medieval church domains of Europe.

Priests were an abiding feature of ancient Egyptian society: there were so many gods, both local deities in particular places and national gods like Re and Osiris, and every god needed his little band of servants (the great gods were served by larger teams). In Sumer, the temples and the priests preceded the kings as leaders of society, but in Egypt there was never any question of a priesthood outdoing pharaoh, who was himself a god. Only at the end of Ramesside times did a high-priest of Amun challenge the rule of the pharaohs. Nevertheless the priests of the larger and more sophisticated cults, especially in Heliopolis and Memphis, constituted the intellectual élite of ancient Egyptian society.

As well as pharaoh and priesthood, nobles and wealthy men owned land in ancient Egypt which they were able to leave to their children and on which they paid taxes. The collection of these taxes was the occasion for the existence of the great body of professional scribes, the bureaucracy of ancient Egypt. There was no money as such, in the form of concrete tokens with agreed values; payments were made in kind, but assessed according to an abstract unit of value that was not made into an independent coinage in its own right. Private land-owners organized and 'employed' the local 'fellaheen', a peasant class that has always existed in Egypt down to modern times. 'Fellah' is an Arabic word meaning 'tiller' and perfectly suits the ancient as well as the modern peasant, who then as now not only tilled the land but was available, as and when need and opportunity arose, for any job to hand.

Pharaoh was the king-pin of society. One of his designations makes him the 'perfect god', and under his rule ancient Egypt functioned not as a modern secular state but as a god-made land. At the 'First Time' (as the Egyptians called the beginning of things), Egypt had been created by God and ruled by God: the living kings who ruled subsequently were the sons and incarnations of God. It is as well to speak of 'God', since behind their multitude of divine personifications the Egyptians often conceived of a generalized divine entity which manifested itself in a thousand different ways. Of course, in everyday terms, kings were the sons of human beings, often—though not always—of the previous king. While descent was through the 'Great Royal Wife' of the former king or through some female related to him, in fact the throne was very often passed on from father to son. But parallel with the human process of conception and birth, the ancient Egyptians imagined for their kings a similar but divine process of events. While some human father, who may not have been the present king, was impregnating the mother of the ruler-to-be, on the divine plane the god was fathering upon the same woman his own divinely conceived son and incarnation. The same idea is expressed in some other religions

Hatshepsut's mother is led into the birth-chamber—a scene from the reliefs depicting Hatshepsut's 'divine birth'.

and goes back in Egypt into Old Kingdom times, but is vividly depicted on the walls of queen Hatshepsut's New Kingdom terraced temple at Deir el-Bahri. In the series of murals there, the fashioning of the spirits of Hatshepsut is recorded, the good-tidings of her impending birth are brought to her mother by the god's messenger Thoth, the mother is led into the birth-chamber by animal-headed gods, the cow-headed goddess Hathor serves as wet-nurse to the new born Hatshepsut, and finally this future divine ruler of the earth is kissed in recognition by Amun himself in the presence of the gods. The whole series rubs in the official conviction that the accession of a new pharaoh to rule on earth was not a merely earthly event but a piece of parallel action in accord with divine happenings. It would probably be true to say that the ancient Egyptians lacked the concept of purely secular occurrences, since in their minds all events took place on the divine as well as human plane: indeed those two planes were quite interwoven.

The notion that pharaoh was a god, whose birth and rule were part of the divine fabric of the cosmos, prevented the institution of kingship from being conceived of merely as a despotism. Since the cosmos was itself a righteous process, then so must be the earthly rule of pharaoh. The New Kingdom court official Rekhmire asks rhetorically: 'what is the king of Upper and Lower Egypt?' and supplies the answer: 'He is a god by whose dealings one lives, the father and mother of all men . . .' In his divinity, the king could shed some of the trappings of mere personal individuality; perhaps that is why statues, reliefs and paintings of pharaoh sometimes tend towards a monumental loss of idiosyncrasy in the direction of strongly idealized depictions. What interested the Egyptians about their world, and consequently about their kings, was not the things that change with changing generations but the things that remain in common between all aspects of the world and its rulers. This justifies us very much in using 'pharaoh' without the definite article to designate the ruler of ancient Egypt at all times, in preference to *the* king: 'pharaoh' is the appropriate generalization. When pharaoh, whether on a tiny early dynastic plaquette in the British Museum or in giant relief on a temple wall at Karnak smites his enemies with one upraised arm, while the other grasps the tops of their heads, he does so without strain and tension as though this was the most natural and easy thing in the world. In other words, he is fulfilling his natural role as earthly god in the grand divine design of the cosmos.

It is essential to absorb, to some extent at least, these unfamiliar concepts of society in order to understand the Egyptian way of doing things: unless we appreciate that other values and other beliefs than our own were at work there, we shall not do justice to the spirit of the ancient Egyptians. But we must equally guard against too 'mythic' an interpretation of this ancient culture, which would lift the whole course of Egyptian life on to an idealized plane without contact with the real world.

Right *The expansionist pharaoh Tuthmosis III, of about 1450 BC, smiting his enemies. Compare this figure with king Den (page 82) posed in exactly the same way some 1,500 years earlier.*

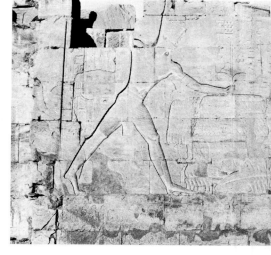

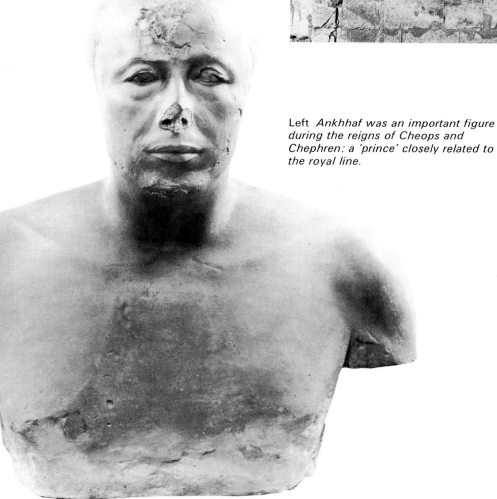

Left *Ankhhaf was an important figure during the reigns of Cheops and Chephren: a 'prince' closely related to the royal line.*

120

The ancient Egyptians, whilst adhering to a system of beliefs very different from our own, were as human and humanly gifted as we are. The stories that Herodotus heard in Egypt reveal that common gossip was not always too loftily related to the grand religious concepts—certainly not in Herodotus's time, and almost certainly not in earlier days either. Rumour had it that Cheops was a wicked and profligate king, with no respect for the gods whose temples he robbed, who set up his own daughter in a brothel to keep the money pouring in for his pyramid project. Another popular story about Cheops cast him in the role later ascribed to Herod. According to this tale, the daughter of a priestly family was visited by Re during the reign of Cheops and conceived three sons. A wise man divined that these three boys would one day rule Egypt and Cheops, when he heard about it, tried to seize the children and remove the threat— unsuccessfully, as it turned out, as with Herod.

The stories about Cheops do at least show that there was a standard to which the behaviour of pharaoh was expected to conform. The key concept here is expressed in the ancient Egyptian word 'Maat'. 'Maat', sometimes personified as a goddess, was one of the special manifestations of God that even Akhenaten was not prepared to assault in favour of his single sun deity. 'Maat' means something like 'correctness' and 'righteous-ness', or 'truth'. But its meaning is not restricted simply to proper be-haviour, or factual veracity, because the Egyptians did not choose to disentangle the nowadays separated concepts of truth, good order, cosmic purpose, fitting conduct and so on to which we resort in order to assemble an impression of what they meant by this single word. 'Maat' was all-important to the ancient Egyptians, the thread that drew together all the divinely-ordained processes of the world, and pharaoh—'the father and mother of all men'—was expected to rule in accordance with 'Maat'. So were his subordinates in positions of power and trust up and down Egypt. There were no codified systems of law and no drawn-up statutes that objectified the procedures to be adopted, but government was ex-pected to be conducted within the requirements of 'Maat'. A piece of popular literature called 'The Tale of the Eloquent Peasant' tells of a wronged 'fellah' (one of the humblest in the land) putting his case against a high official in no uncertain terms, confident he can demonstrate that he has not received his due—in other words, has not been treated in accordance with the rules of 'Maat'. The universal acceptance of the concept of 'Maat' put a brake in real terms upon the powers of the divinely sanctioned king and his officials.

The subordinates who governed under pharaoh seem preponderantly to have been his own family and relatives in early times and this situation was maintained throughout the Old Kingdom, though families of nobles and provincial governors were also powerful. A son of Cheops named Hemon is thought to have been the architect of his father's pyramid and

Ankhhaf was another such closely related big-wig during the reigns of Cheops and Chephren. Councils of royal 'princes' and nobles assisted the king in his governmental decisions—accounts of their deliberations are surely misleading in representing pharaoh as the only active voice in these councils, with the rest seemingly only present to agree with him! We can be sure that some very important officials were able to set their stamp upon affairs from the first, even in the shadow of the divine king. Djoser's 'chancellor' Imhotep must have been one such, who pioneered the massive use of stone in the Step Pyramid complex of Sakkara and was deified in later centuries as a god of medicine. Imhotep seems to have been a high priest of Re at Heliopolis (near Cairo) and we may be certain that such priests, who might be said to have been the dons of the world's first universities, were immensely learned and capable men and adroit not merely in the religious complexities of their civilization but also in practical affairs like astronomy and geometry. Star-watching was probably more significant in all ancient cultures than we have been accustomed to think, for it made possible the determination of seasonal time-keeping and the confident orientation of structures; while the measuring-out of fields and land plots after inundations of the Nile made geometry an important study. It is not surprising, therefore, that the priests of Re should have been so vital to the running of the country and the organization of state projects. Manetho, who wrote the 'Egyptian Memoirs' whose fragments have proved so important in reconstructing Egyptian history, was himself a high priest of Re at Heliopolis in Ptolemaic times.

The most important post under the king from Archaic times onwards was the one that Egyptologists render by the term 'vizier', which perhaps has too many 'Arabian Nights' connotations to be entirely suitable. The vizier undertook the daily affairs of the divine ruler and himself controlled an ever-increasing body of lesser officials. The bureaucracy under the vizier was greatly expanded, first in Middle Kingdom times and then again when the New Kingdom changed the character of ancient Egyptian society in the direction of more imperial and military offices. Always, however, the vizier stood at the head of this hierarchy of officials: to the vizier Rekhmire, who described the king as 'father and mother of all men', a New Kingdom pharaoh exclaimed: 'Look to the office; be vigilant about it, for it is the mainstay of the whole land'.

The tendency during Egyptian history was for the offices in pharaoh's service to drift out of the hands of his own near relatives and into the possession of sometimes quite humble men who constituted a sort of 'meritocracy'. After the end of Old Kingdom times, the bureaucracy had in general a non-royal character, but the meritocrats were inclined to want to pass on their offices to their own sons and a new sort of inherited structure came into being. During the Second Intermediate Period, offices were even sold and a legal case is on record as having been brought

Gold was used in the manufacture of royal insignia and high military honours: these great gold flies were apparently awarded as medals for valour to queen Aahotep for her part in ridding Egypt of the Hyksos usurpers at the beginning of the New Kingdom.

Next page The gigantic constructions of Ramesses II, like the columns of the Hypostyle Hall at Karnak, show that the New Kingdom was capable of building on a scale of massiveness comparable with the achievements of the Pyramid Age, in quantity if not in quality. The original paintwork has brilliantly survived under the lintel.

against a seller who wouldn't relinquish the post in question to the buyer! Unlike the modern world, in which men usually make careers within the structure of a single profession, Egyptian officials were quite versatile as to actual posts, and careers were made by moving through a variety of jobs, rather in the way that cabinet ministers do it in Britain today.

The regional organization of Egyptian society was always very distinct. To begin with, there was the traditional division of the country into the Two Lands of Lower and Upper Egypt. For the purposes of administration, Upper Egypt was further divided into twenty-two provinces which are usually called 'nomes' (after a Greek word) and Lower Egypt into sixteen such nomes in Middle Kingdom times, rising to twenty-two like Upper Egypt by the end of ancient Egyptian history. These nomes possessed proudly proclaimed individual identities with nome emblems rather like modern flags and nome governors, called after the Greek 'nomarchs'. Old Memphis, 'White Walls' or simply 'The Wall' as the Egyptians often called it, was a nome with a nomarch of its own. These nomarchs were appointed by the king, but the appointees were usually local worthies in stable times. One of their chief duties was to collect taxes. In times of trouble, there was always a tendency for Egypt to lapse into the system of local independencies out of which it had been created. Nomes fell out with one another and even fought, until central authority was re-asserted.

Nome standards.

During Old Kingdom times, what fighting had to be done was conducted with locally raised forces, conscripted for the matter in hand such as putting down the Nubian or Libyan neighbours of ancient Egypt or collecting tribute from them. The raising of such emergency militia was left to the local governors and nomarchs. The king kept his own palace guard and was, at least formally, commander-in-chief of all Egyptian forces. He also controlled special contingents who were sent on mining expeditions into the desert to quarry the minerals that belonged to him alone. But the king not only owned the Egyptian land and all its resources, he could truthfully anticipate the assurance that Ivan the Terrible of Russia sent to Queen Elizabeth: 'I am the only merchant in Muscovy'. Pharaoh was the only merchant in Egypt, at least during Old and Middle Kingdom times, and he sent other special forces to conduct trade with remoter foreign lands like Punt. These forces were organized and disciplined in a military fashion. Free-enterprise merchants operating in an independent way only really became established during the New Kingdom and then they required licenses under pharaoh's authority.

Though the Old Kingdom had no need of large standing armies, since it lacked imperial designs upon its neighbours and was not exposed to the threat of invasion from any of them, such forces as it did possess were quite tightly structured and disciplined. There were daily parades and the military 'rule-books' laid down requirements of conduct for the soldiery, putting some emphasis on relations with the civilian citizenry of Egypt, who were not to be plundered by the army. When the Old Kingdom went down in anarchy during the First Intermediate Period, the local barons who usurped the king's central power in their own fiefdoms raised their own forces for offensive and defensive purposes, sometimes recruiting foreign mercenaries to aid their designs. The Middle Kingdom rulers who re-established central authority built on these local armies and extended their personal guards and contingents to create the first imperial armed forces. A set of model soldiers from a tomb of the First Intermediate Period in Middle Egypt shows the sort of combined Egyptian and foreign (in this case Nubian) forces that existed at this time: the reddish Egyptians carry hide shields and long spears, while the darker Nubians are armed only with bows.

As we would expect, it was the imperialist New Kingdom that saw the development of a standing army of professional soldiery, with a proper system of ranks. The post of 'Great General' stood at the top of the military hierarchy and the man who filled it was a very important figure in Egyptian society. Akhenaten's (and Tutankhamun's) general Horemheb eventually took supreme power as pharaoh at the end of the Eighteenth Dynasty and the whole line of Nineteenth Dynasty Ramesside rulers was founded by an army man. The armies they commanded were highly organized and were drilled, on the parade ground and in battle, to the sound of the trumpet—military trumpets were among the gear stowed in Tutankhamun's tomb. Foreign mercenaries were more and more relied upon to supplement the native Egyptian forces in New Kingdom times— in fact prisoners were very much 'pressed' into service. Life in the army could be hard going for Egyptian and foreigner alike, as some ancient texts proclaim: 'He is taken off and put in camp. He has brackish water to drink and only stops marching to mount guard. When he reaches the enemy, he is like a snared bird with no strength left in his body. When he gets back to Egypt he is like worm-eaten wood. He falls ill and is brought back on a donkey. His clothes are stolen and his servant runs away'. But in fact soldiering could bring real rewards in terms of social preferment for the Egyptian, and settled luxury for the foreign mercenary: 'Bows and weapons stayed in store and they and their wives and children ate and drank their fill'.

Above *This group of fighting men comes from a Middle Kingdom tomb.*

Below *One of these trumpets from the tomb of Tutankhamun was played and recorded in the 1930's, producing a very martial sound.*

Above left *Tutankhamun took to his grave a writing kit, including pencase and papyrus-smoother: Egyptian pharaohs, unlike some barbarian rulers of early feudal Europe, valued the art of writing.*

Although a systematic body of law as such did not exist in ancient Egypt and all things were judged according to 'Maat' and one might say 'common sense', there were instead professional judges and police to enforce 'law and order'. The police existed as part of the armed forces from Old Kingdom times on and were given a distinctive quality in the Middle Kingdom when many desert Nubians from the south were enrolled. Legal actions of various sorts are recorded: there is an account of the trial of some tomb robbers who had been raiding royal tombs at Thebes in the Late New Kingdom. Juries might consist of both professional judges and local worthies, local governors and indeed any respectable citizens. 'Higher courts' were available in the persons of the vizier and pharaoh himself. The commonest form of punishment seems to have been a beating with a stick: it is illustrated, for example, in the tomb of the noble Menna at Thebes, where a peasant is shown being belaboured. Like the Romans, the Egyptians sometimes regarded a good beating as a necessary encouragement of courtroom truthfulness among the lower classes. Forced labour, mutilation, caging in wooden frames, exile and death were also forms of punishment.

The 'civil service' which kept Egyptian society running on a day-to-day basis was made up of technical experts, like the engineers and builders who designed and supervised projects for which the 'fellaheen' supplied the work force, and the army of scribes who communicated affairs up and down the country and recorded and accounted for everything that went on. The scribe's vocation was a valued one and the ancient Egyptians had none of that contempt for reading and writing that the barbarian rulers of early feudal Europe displayed. The young Tutankhamun took with him into his tomb a scribe's kit of pencase, writing-palettes, and papyrus burnisher (which was used to smooth out the surface of the writing material), and king Wenis, nearly two thousand years before Tutankhamun, included this declaration in his pyramid texts: 'I sit before Re. I open his portfolios. I break the seals of his decrees and seal up his despatches. I send forth his tireless runners. I do whatever he dictates to me'. Evidently the Egyptian kings were not afraid to be caught capable of writing, unlike some of their medieval counterparts who left that sort of thing to humble clerks.

Egyptian culture in any case held the very idea of writing in high esteem. Just as the representation of a man in stone somehow immortalized him, so the rendering of ideas and assertions in the form of written signs somehow objectified them and made them real in a grander way than merely saying them. Especially when writing took the form of imperishably carved hieroglyphs did the Egyptians respect it. The more everyday 'longhand' hieratic and later demotic probably lacked some of this force, and of course these forms were more often committed to less permanent materials like wood or papyrus.

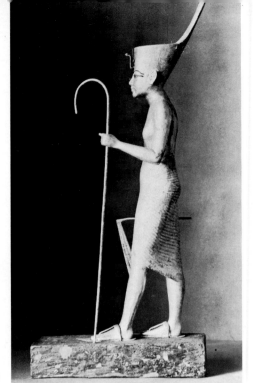

Right *A little gilded figure of Tutankhamun from his tomb shows him in the role of the good shepherd of his people.*

Below *Scribes were on hand to record and tabulate every aspect of Egyptian life: in the fields, the courts, the offices, at the sites of public works and building operations.*

Above all, writing was absolutely *necessary* to ancient Egypt. That is almost certainly the reason why it came to be invented and developed — and not just in Egypt, but also in Sumer and all the other cultural centres. Writing whenever it occurs is not at first employed for purposes of literature, but really for purposes of recording: lists of goods, accounts, simple directions, marks of ownership, and magical formulae of the sort that are closely bound up with everyday affairs are the first uses made of writing. In Egypt, the highly centralized structure of society where pharaoh's rule extended all the length of a long country required an efficient means of communication and record keeping. The development of Egyptian society and the development of the role of the scribes went hand in hand and at the same time both required each other and made each other possible. Writing, of course, occurs in some form from the very beginning of Egyptian dynastic history.

Writing is inscribed all over ancient Egyptian monuments, but the 'civil service' scribes wrote mostly on papyrus in ink with reed or rush pens. They also used leather from time to time or inscribed their writing on wooden palettes, and international correspondence (at least in New Kingdom times) was conducted on clay tablets impressed with the wedge-writing of Akkadian cuneiform. Papyrus, however, was the chief medium and its invention was one of the great technical achievements of ancient Egypt. Thickets of the papyrus plant grew lushly all over Egypt in historical times (today it only occurs in the far southern reaches of the Nile) and the tall stems of the plant were collected on an industrial scale to manufacture 'paper'. The process of paper-making by means of papyrus was a simple if time-consuming one. The stalks, about an inch in diameter, were cut into regularized lengths and peeled. Then they were split vertically into thin strips. A square of these were laid down upon a board and across them was set another square with its strips running at right angles. Perhaps more layers were added. Then the sandwich of papyrus strips was bonded together by pounding with a wooden mallet until the layers were tightly compacted and a thin sheet was produced. No glue or bonding agent was necessary since the surface texture of the papyrus strips themselves effected a natural interlocking of the layers. It would seem, from the carrying out of modern experiments, that quite a long period of pounding was required. Extended strips of papyrus could be manufactured by pounding together the edges of separate sheets. Finally, the surface of the paper required finishing by means of round-headed smoothing tools to make it fit for the pen to run over it.

A great mass of written papyri has survived from ancient Egypt, particularly from New Kingdom and later times. Even so, the quantity of papyrus employed in ancient Egypt must have been a thousand times greater than what has come down to us. It seems that great store-rooms of papyri were maintained, like huge civil service memo banks. It is not difficult to see how these enormous piles of paper work were created, for from the Old Kingdom to the New the tombs of the nobles show scribes in action at the scene of every aspect of ancient Egyptian life. In the Old Kingdom tomb of Ti at Sakkara, scribes are depicted at work in their offices with their papyrus rolls and writing-kits; in the New Kingdom tomb of Menna at Thebes, scribes are painted at work in the fields recording the yield of the crops. In the Brooklyn Museum there is a papyrus from about 1150 BC full of terrific details of land-ownership, crop-yields, taxes and plot-cultivation. An ancient text declares in sober truth: 'It is the scribe who assesses and collects the taxes in Upper and Lower Egypt. It is he who governs the entire country and every affair is under his control'.

Scribes were trained in special schools and a great deal of copying of model texts was involved, rather in the way that 'copper plate' copying was emphasized in our schools right into this century. The copying was not done on valuable papyrus but often on scraps of wood or pottery, and examples of the work of pupils, with the teacher's corrections marked upon them, have survived. Naturally, in the course of copying model texts, the pupil scribe acquired a great deal of familiarity with the literature of his culture and knowledge of the rest of the school subjects.

Many statues in scribes' garb have been found in the tombs of high officials and some of them are very fine: frequently the subject is shown squatting crosslegged with his kilt drawn tight across his knees as a platform for his papyrus roll, and his writing-hand formed to hold his pen. One of the very best of these statues, which well expresses the confidence and intelligence of this all-important section of the ancient Egyptian community, is the 'scribe accroupi' in the Louvre in Paris.

At the bottom of the social scale were the peasant farmers whom it is convenient to call 'fellaheen'. They were not slaves and in general Egypt was not a slave-owning society: certainly not in the sense that a large body of slaves was required to keep the society going, as was the case with ancient Rome; there were slaves, war-captives perhaps, in Egypt and there were more of them in imperial New Kingdom times than before, but they were not the economic backbone of society. Something like the serf system of medieval Europe or later Russia probably corresponds best to the situation in which the Egyptian peasants found themselves. They were certainly attached at all times to some great power, like the pharaoh's own administration or the estate of a prince or the fief of a temple, and they were continuously liable to be enrolled in projects which took them away from their own patches, like pyramid-building or canal-digging. Their protection was the emphasis upon 'Maat' which was supposed to govern all dealings in the world, but whether this was always any better applied than the Christian principles of the medieval barons of Europe is open to doubt. There are records of several occasions when strikes took place among the workforce labouring on the royal tombs in the Valley of the Kings during the reign of Ramesses III, around 1160 BC. These strikes were over official delays in the distribution of rations: 'We are hungry, eighteen days of this month have already gone by'; 'We have no clothes, no fat, no fish and no vegetables. Write this to pharaoh, our good Lord, write to the vizier, our chief, so that we may be given the means to live'. Because these men, who lived in the workmen's village at Deir el-Medina on the West Bank at Thebes, were engaged on a royal project, they were able to exert an amount of leverage on their rulers to obtain their due. The same may not have been true of the ordinary 'fellaheen' of ancient Egypt.

The position of women in ancient Egyptian society was rather more modern in character than that of other civilizations of the ancient world, contrasting with the gynaeceum situation of the Greeks (which was in line with the strict meaning of the Arabic 'harem', 'a place set apart'). In this respect, ancient Egyptian society has been compared with bourgeois Europe of the nineteenth century, which it may in some ways have surpassed: women had equal rights at law and were accorded the same prospects in the next world; they could occupy certain official posts in the food and clothing industries. Three or four of Egypt's pharaohs were women— Hatshepsut of the Eighteenth Dynasty being the best known case—and women served as priestesses in some of the ancient cults. It is not altogether true to say, by the way, that Egypt was a matrilineal society with descent and inheritance solely in the female line: matrilineal codes existed through-out Egyptian history but both in royal terms and among the professional classes inheritance was usually from father to son. Marriage and monogamy seem to have been the rule in ancient Egypt and, before Ptolemaic times, there is little evidence of brother-sister marriages of the sort popularly imputed to the Egyptians. Kings married their sisters in a matrilineal spirit but they were exceptional cases who in any case had whole harems of queens and concubines, acquired as much for diplomatic reasons as for luxury. The family among the ancient Egyptians does not seem to have been the complexly ramified system of relationships encountered by anthropologists among so-called 'primitive' peoples. There are fewer words for degrees of family relationship in ancient Egyptian than in basic Indo-European. The Egyptians in fact were not unlike modern western societies in neglecting to keep track of relationships beyond the immediate family unit. Divorce was recognized, and men paid compensation for the privilege. The penalties for wifely adultery seem to have been as severe as they traditionally have been in some Moslem countries until the present day. Not a great deal is known about Egyptian sexual mores, though love-poems of the Late Period express passionate individual attachments and popular stories, even religious myths, sometimes cast the gods in a scandalous light by recent standards. Homosexuality was occasionally imputed to some of the gods, but as far as we can tell was not a common social habit in the way that it was in classical Greece, where of course, attitudes to women were much more 'oriental' than in Egypt.

But what really distinguishes Egyptian society from the rest of the civilizations of the ancient world is the institution of divine kingship which united a whole land while other countries remained as often as not just collections of warring city-states.

In Sumer, for example, the institution of kingship evolved by a gradual emphasis upon hereditary power out of rather 'democratic' origins; and the Sumerian kings never figured as such divinely powerful rulers as the pharaohs of Egypt. Strong central rule did not come so early to Mesopotamia as it did to Egypt. The Roman emperors, by way of Alexander's example modelled upon the Persian autocracy and the Egyptian divine kingship, revived the pretensions of the pharaohs and bequeathed something of their pretensions to the popes of medieval Europe. A little gilded wooden figure of Tutankhamun from his tomb in the Valley of the Kings vividly realizes the pharaoh's claim to be the good shepherd of his flock: he carries, in addition to the kilt and sandles worn by his 'fellow men', the shepherd's crook and so-called flail (for gathering a natural gum that exuded from some of the bushes of the pasture) that symbolize his pastoral origins as the guarantor of his people's well-being.

Chapter VII Everyday Life and Life after Death

It has already been indicated that the better part of Egyptian archaeology is inevitably concerned with the mortuary remains of this ancient civilization. This situation arises out of the related facts that the ancient Egyptians endowed their funerary monuments with the permanence of stone construction, meant to last for ever and not to perish as they were content to see their everyday homes do, and that—at least in Upper Egypt— their tombs were not built in the flooded valley where they would sink below the water-table but up on the edge of the desert out of reach of the river. So that, in reconstructing everyday life, archaeology must largely rely on the evidence that comes from the paintings and models in their tombs. But there is another good reason why it is worth bringing together the everyday life of the Egyptians with their beliefs and practices to do with the after-life: the ancient Egyptians, more vividly than any other culture, regarded life and after-life as absolutely indivisible and in many ways as a matter of simple continuity in a single universe which embraced the so-called living and dead without distinction. It would be to oversimplify to say that for the ancient Egyptians the after-life meant only a straight continuation of life on earth, writ large perhaps in terms of good health and plenty, but certainly there is one level of their belief at which such an Elysian fancy holds good. Scenes in the tomb of Sennedjem, in the cemetery at Deir el-Medina of New Kingdom artists and craftsmen who laboured on the royal monuments in the nearby Valley of the Kings, show the dead man and his wife pursuing just such a straightforward extension of their daily lives in the hereafter, sowing and reaping a bumper crop of corn and enjoying every sort of agricultural prosperity. In the case of such a relatively simple pair as Sennedjem and his wife, the motive for these depictions may have been a sort of celebratory optimism about the hereafter; but there exists from Old Kingdom times onwards an aspect of

Above *In an Old Kingdom tomb relief, herdsmen guide their charges home across a stream.*

Below *The vineyards of ancient Egypt produced wines that were 'bottled' and 'labelled' in a very modern fashion.*

136

magic about the way in which the scenes of the daily round are recorded in the tomb paintings and in the models that have, in some cases, survived. If on one level life was to continue after death on the same pattern as every-day existence, then obviously there were not only the fruits of life to be enjoyed in the hereafter but there was work to be done. The tomb paintings and models demonstrate the magical intention both to ensure the enjoy-ment of the good things of the after-life and to compel the undertaking of all the work that would be as necessary in the next life as in this one. In line with the social divisions of ancient Egypt, it was not to be assumed in the case of the kings and nobles that they would do the work themselves so the scenes and models in their tombs provide a host of servants to see to these things. In an extension of egalitarian attitudes, the tombs of folk of the more ordinary sort sometimes took up the idea of substitute toilers in the form of model figures to shoulder the burdens of the after-life. As in all cases where artistic creation is applied to the expression of magical or religious or philosophical ideas, it is not always useful to try to distinguish between the ideological purposes in question and the exuberant artistic manifestation of them which draws upon and appeals to universally human capabilities. At any rate thanks to these aspects of ancient Egyptian belief about the after-life, which led them so vividly to depict in their tombs the real life they knew on earth, a very detailed and highly coloured picture has come down to us of the everyday lives of these people.

As is already clear from consideration of their Nile Valley environ-ment and the early stages of their civilization, the Egyptians were farmers before they were anything else. Farming remained the basis of their culture—and the chief occupation of most of its citizens—from the days before the Two Lands were united until Roman times, when Egypt became an imperial granary for its foreign rulers, and indeed right down to the present day. The tomb-scenes of the Old Kingdom nobles at Sakkara and the New Kingdom nobles at Thebes exhaustively illustrate the range of farming activities: sowing and reaping the corn, winnowing the grain, growing vegetables like lettuces and cucumbers, tending fruit-trees like figs and pomegranates (there were no New World potatoes and tomatoes, and no apples, oranges or pears while honey was used for sweetening in the absence of sugar-cane), herding cattle and goats, keeping geese and catching wild birds in cages (there were no camels in historical Egypt until Arab times, though evolving forms of camel had lived much earlier in Africa). Although the old pre-farming life of hunting and gathering did persist on the fringes of ancient Egypt and a purer pastoralism was practised by nomadic neighbours, the solid peasant citizenry of Egypt was engaged upon precisely the style of life that these tomb scenes illustrate. And, though there were lean years when low Niles failed to fertilize as much land as was required and people went hungry, everyday subsistence on the basis of Egypt's farming production was usually pretty well assured.

But because the tomb scenes upon which we rely belong to well-placed nobles for the most part, the diet of the ancient Egyptians is apt to look richer and more varied than it really was for the average citizen. Along with the depicted requirements in the way of clothes and ointments that the wealthy Egyptians recorded in their tombs, they also had written out and illustrated whole 'menus' for the after-life which no doubt do not greatly exaggerate the standard of living to which they were accustomed from day to day. These 'menus' call for various sorts of bread and cakes, joints of meat, poultry, fruits and vegetables. All this was to be washed down with wines and beers: wine-making is illustrated in several New Kingdom tomb paintings where all stages of the process from gathering, through treading to 'bottling' are recorded; wines were even 'labelled' with little dockets giving their provenance and vintage and distinguished as good or indifferent. The staple diet of the Egyptians was a good deal simpler than these elaborate and hopeful menus suggest—bread, beer, and onions, with some meat if one was lucky, always constituted a good enough meal (beef especially was probably outside the daily expectations of the average Egyptian, though poultry and pigeons were commoner). Fish from the Nile provided a plentiful source of food for common folk though it was somewhat despised by the better-off and never offered to the dead or to the gods. Beer was the standard ancient Egyptian tipple, being brewed as a by-product of bread-making. Partly-baked cakes were broken up and fermented in jars and the result, a rather weak potion, probably resembled the native beers that are still produced in the Sudan and Ethiopia. Recent experiments in reproducing the ancient brewing process lead this writer to conclude that ancient Egyptian beer must have been something of an acquired taste. Strong beers do not, of course, go well with hot climates so the ancient brew was probably a welcome one for peasants who toiled under the sun. Even so, drunkenness was a re-cognized problem in ancient Egypt and there are strictures recorded against over-indulgence: 'you speak and an unintelligible utterance comes forth . . . you are found helpless on the ground like a little child'.

Fragments of food from Egyptian tombs have been preserved, either in the form of provisions for the dead or as the remains of funerary repasts taken by mourners at the tomb. There are bits of poultry, probably grilled or roasted, and the dried-up remains of fruits (eaten raw) and cakes. Examination of the fairly numerous bits of bread from ancient Egypt confirms what the frequently worn-down teeth of mummies tell us: that sand was an ever-present and unavoidable feature of their diet! Consequently dental trouble was a common complaint among the ancient Egyptians.

The fact of mummification and the high incidence of physical preser-vation adds an unusual dimension to our knowledge of the daily life of ancient Egypt: more medical knowledge is available about the Egyptians than about any other peoples of the ancient world. Mummification was

Above *The outer faces of some sarcophagi mimic the appearance of the façades of the houses of the living.*

Below *Egyptian tombs sometimes contain models of everyday scenes, like this little granary.*

itself, however, a partly destructive process in that internal organs were removed and separately preserved and a good deal of medical investigation is debarred. Nevertheless, such gross physical features as club-footedness or death as the result of grievous bodily harm are often identified. Tuberculosis in the form of Pott's disease, where destruction of vertebrae and spinal deformation occur, has been identified in the mummy of a Twenty-first Dynasty priest—lung tuberculosis cannot be identified because lungs were removed in mummification. Blood-grouping is a technique that has been applied with spectacular success to the mummies of Tutankhamun and an individual from a nearby tomb, whereby close blood-brotherhood was demonstrated for these two. Methods are currently being devised to make possible the temporary reconstitution of tissues from mummies and new medical knowledge may well result from this work. Ill health and limited life-expectancy have always been the human norms outside modern industrialized states: Egypt was probably more fortunate than most ancient civilizations in this respect because of its natural abundance and favourable climate but even here the average life expectancy for a population probably smaller than London's today was about forty years and (because the physical remains mostly belong to the upper reaches of society) quite probably a lot shorter for the peasant class.

Egypt's climate is an agreeable one in most parts of the country for most of the year: in winter, Lower Egypt may be wet and cool at times and in summer Upper Egypt can be unbearably hot. But for much of the year it is possible even to sleep out in the fields with only rudimentary shelter. The homes of the ancient Egyptians were built out of mud and mud-brick, with limited use of timber which was scarce and not very suited to constructional purposes. The homes of the farm labourers must have been extremely simple affairs, moulded up out of mud like the houses that can still be seen out in the fields of Egypt today. Farm buildings would have been similarly constructed and there are tomb models showing farmyards and granaries that do not differ from present day examples. The homes of the more privileged sections of society reached levels of considerable sophistication, with ornamental gardens and garden pools, but once again perishable materials were employed, in this case bricks made by mixing straw into mud. Walls made from such bricks were plastered over and painted with vivid designs, to judge from the fragments that have survived. Because of the nature of everyday building and its location in the valley we shall never be able to visit an ancient Egyptian Pompeii with extensively surviving domestic architecture. The most that is left to us consists of mud-brick foundations, like those of Akhenaten's new capital at Amarna, which can be reconstructed on paper by archaeologists, and occasional representations in tomb art or actual realizations in mortuary stone of what the impermanent houses of the living looked like. Djoser's complex at Sakkara is an outstanding example of this procedure, with its stone representations of wicker fencing and roof beams and other wooden prototypes. Indeed, Djoser's Step Pyramid complex quite probably bears a strong resemblance in principle if not in all details to his living palace down below the desert escarpment in the green valley location of 'White Walls' or Memphis. This palace, like its funerary counterpart, must have had its halls and store-chambers, its gated entrances and encircling wall. In the same way the panelled façades of the houses of the richer dead seem to be reproduced in some of the sarcophagi of the Old Kingdom.

The tomb art, apart from the models, does not depict much in the way of architectural features but it does convey a great deal of information about ancient Egyptian dress, as do the statues of the dead. Additionally, a certain amount of actual fabric has survived and some complete garments, like the sailor's leather kilt in the Boston Museum with its patch. Skins must have been the earliest Egyptian form of clothing in predynastic times and the skin of one animal in particular, the leopard, went on being worn— in a spirit of religious conservatism—as part of the ceremonial priestly costume until the last days of ancient Egypt. The historical Egyptians were great exponents of spinning and weaving linen cloth (although they are also known to have worn woollen clothes) and the tools of the trade that have survived, as well as the wall paintings, show that their techniques differed little from the traditional crafts of today.

The basic dress of the two sexes was from earliest times: for the man, a kilt-like girdle around the waist which did not reach the knees and was fastened by a knot in front; for the woman, a long dress covering the whole body from the shoulders to the ankles. The famous statue of prince Rahotep and wife, of the Fourth Dynasty, in the Cairo Museum shows a pair dressed in this way. People engaged in any sort of manual labour, including girls working in the corn fields, went practically naked, and the ordinary Egyptian continued to wear the short kilt throughout Egyptian history. The nobles of the Old Kingdom gradually adopted a fuller form of kilt however. Women in Old Kingdom times wore remarkably plain dresses for the most part, usually white in colour. In the Middle Kingdom, progress in cloth-making led to the adoption among the upper classes of very fine and virtually transparent dress (with short kilts beneath for the men, while the women's clothes were also more elaborately decorated). During the New Kingdom, when Egyptian society underwent considerable changes as a result of wider foreign contacts and imperial wealth, dress was influenced by the fashions of the neighbouring peoples and became richly elaborated. The male nobles now wore a sort of cape over the shoulders and the outer kilt was lengthened and cut away at the front; their women turned to two-piece costumes where a wide outer garment knotted over one shoulder covered a close-fitting tunic underneath. Embroidery in gold and silver and coloured threads was applied, after the pattern of the more flamboyant western Asiatic styles. Jewellery was worn by both sexes—rings, bracelets, necklaces and, in the New Kingdom, ear-rings. A pair belonging to Tutankhamun was found in his tomb. As for head and feet, the Egyptians went sometimes bare-headed but sometimes sported wigs or folded linen coverings and usually wore sandals of papyrus or leather, fastened by a strap whose characteristic shape ☥ supplied the hieroglyphic system with the 'ankh' sign which also means 'life'. A golden version of such sandals was worn by the mummy of Tutankhamun.

That Elysian after-life, upon whose representations in the tombs of the dead we have been drawing to illustrate the everyday life of the living (because it is patterned so closely upon the real world) was not the ancient Egyptians' only picture of the nature of the hereafter. Latter-day religious systems have put great emphasis upon a coherence and internal self-consistency (not always achieved) that the ancient Egyptians simply felt no need of. It is important to understand that single, exclusive versions of any sort of belief are vanishingly rare in Egyptian philosophical thinking and that, where a multitude of beliefs was current, the Egyptians saw no problems of contradiction. It is tempting to see in their multiplicity of approaches towards the central problems of life a modern sort of metaphysical thinking like that proposed by some advanced theologians of our own time, but it is equally doubtful whether the concept of metaphor in these matters would have meant much, even to those sophisticated priests who wrestled with the theological systems of ancient Egypt. The beliefs of ancient Egypt no doubt arose in a multitude of centres in predynastic times when small and slightly differentiated communities were living without political unity along the Nile, and these separate centres were able to contribute quite different versions of various beliefs to the religious systems of historical times. Such an explanation supplies a mechanism for the origin of the differing beliefs but goes no way towards answering the question as to why the Egyptians should not have been offended—as we usually are—by the 'contradictions' brought about by the simultaneous currency of those differing beliefs. We must simply face the fact that we are dealing with another culture having different aims and requirements from our own which could derive value from a multiplicity of approaches to such issues as that of life after death.

So it came about that the notion that life after death simply continued, even if writ a little larger and more prosperous, in just the same way as it had already been lived before death was not the one and only way in which the Egyptians regarded the matter. Moreover, at different periods, differing emphasis was given to the various approaches towards the subject of the after-life. The strongly materialistic concept, as we ourselves might choose to regard it, that the soul remained close to the body lying in its tomb or 'house of eternity' and required the remembrance and everyday attentions of its surviving relatives (or specially appointed priesthoods in

142

Right *Priests continued to wear a leopard-skin robe that must go back to the customs of the earliest Egyptians: here Tutankhamun's successor Ay, in the role of a priest, performs ceremonies before the dead king.*

Below *The Old Kingdom couple Rahotep and his wife wear the standard nobles' costume of the time.*

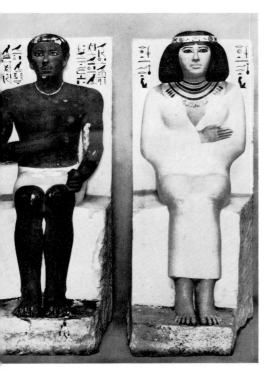

Right *The strap of the sandal, here done in gold for Tutankhamun's mummy, gave to the Egyptians their 'ankh' sign of life.*

the case of very distinguished persons) was never very far away from Egyptian beliefs about the next life. This approach entailed the preservation of the body and its provision with a permanent home where food offerings and other appropriate rituals could be performed. The personal 'soul' of the dead was frequently conceived in the form of a human-headed bird that might fly out of the tomb and about the world during the daytime but would return at night to be close to the preserved physical body of the deceased. This personal 'soul' was called the 'Ba' by the ancient Egyptians and is vividly depicted in some of the New Kingdom artisans' tombs at Thebes. This was the surviving portion of the ancient Egyptian deceased that was endowed with will and individuality. For another aspect of the human being, one which was present from birth and was indestructible but not so personal and individualized, the Egyptians used the word 'Ka': it is really impossible to do better than equate the 'Ka' with some such modern concept as 'life-force' or 'vital energy'. These two more-or-less spiritual entities, the Ba and Ka, do not exhaust the catalogue of the components of the ancient Egyptian human essence—for there were in addition: another invisible power called the 'Akh'; the shadow of a man, depicted as a black figure in the tomb paintings; and also his heart and his name. In line with the Egyptian emphasis upon the magical power of utterance, the naming of the dead was thought to be of great value in preserving his essence after death. We have seen in the case of Akhenaten that erasure of names was a powerful means towards the destruction of one's enemies. Even if we do not pronounce them correctly, we are often fulfilling an eagerly sought-after ancient Egyptian requirement in translating the names of these long-dead persons and writing and talking about them! If it seems at first glance strange that the Egyptians should have maintained a belief in so many apparently distinct elements of the human essence which could act separately in the world and separately survive death, then we should remember that the body-mind-spirit-soul concept has seemed worth the ponderings of a great many of our own civilization's thinkers. It may be that the very notion of a mind-body distinction, still current in our day, will strike our descendants as being every bit as quaint and incomprehensible as the Egyptian ideas may seem to us.

The preservation of the body was a very Egyptian pre-occupation, though it is possible that mummification was in reality more widespread in the ancient world than now appears, for traces of its practice are bound to be rare outside the favourable natural conditions of Egypt where long-term survival of physical remains is common. Natural mummies have occurred in other places—in Andean caves, in Alpine glaciers or even in one instance in a cupboard in Rhyl where a draught of dry air preserved a pensioner's body from decomposition and death-certificate.

Natural mummification was no doubt the precursor of applied mummification. When shallow desert-graves gave way in predynastic times to elaborate chieftains' burials whose coveted grave-goods obliged deeper interment away from the drying sun, then consequent decomposition of the body may well have prompted the Egyptians to have recourse to artificial means of preservation. With time, this came to include long treatment in dessicating natron salts and the removal of the corruptible internal organs. Alongside the efforts put into preserving the body, a second line of defence was devised in the form of life-like statues that would do service for the dead man's survival just as well as his actual body. The statue of Djoser in the booth at the base of his pyramid is an example of this idea.

While all these practices to do with physical survival were being maintained, another set of ancient Egyptian beliefs always took the view that part at least of the dead man's essence quitted the world of the every-day round altogether and became associated with natural phenomena on a far grander scale. According to one standpoint, the dead went to inhabit, or even become one with, those circumpolar stars that never set and therefore seem endowed with a particularly vivid sort of eternity. Another version, which was more widely believed, held that the dead went to journey with the sun (more properly sun-*god*) in his daily crossing of the heavens and night-time sojourn in the underworld. Such beliefs were at first attached to the after-life only of the king himself, whose pre-eminence in the scheme of things merited these exalted prospects. This royal restriction would certainly seem to have obtained in the Old Kingdom and it is tempting to see in the pyramids an expression of the quite particular notion of the after-life that separated kings from nobles and the rest. It is possible that for the toiling mass of ancient Egyptian peasantry no particular vision of an after-life applied at all. In Sumer, and in the later Semitic civilizations of Mesopotamia as in Greece and Rome, the after-life does not seem to have held for any station in life the rosy prospects that it promised the Egyptians and their ruling classes in particular. The pictures in the Old Kingdom tombs of the nobles, especially in the Fifth and Sixth Dynasties, bear witness to the great expectations of their owners. By contrast, the pyramids (and it is particularly striking in the case of the two most imposing ones, of Cheops and Chephren) totally neglected to incorporate any such optimistic and reassuring scenes based upon the everyday life of ancient Egypt, unless these were carried on the now-vanished walls of their causeways. Djoser's pyramid has something in common with the Old Kingdom nobles' tombs in that it shows the king engaged upon some of his worldly activities, but the pyramids of Cheops and Chephren have nothing at all of this. It is as if they fulfill their great purpose simply by being what they are in all their imposing grandeur and simple guise of eternity. These are qualities that they share with the sun and the circumpolar stars and with the rhythm of the seasons in the world of nature. To the peasant farmers toiling in the fields of the green valley below, the looming masses of these royal resting-places up on the desert's edge must have been at one with the rest of the cosmic forces that shaped and supported their entire lives.

The sun-god was often pictured as sailing across the skies in a boat and the king was thought to go to join the crew of that boat, or even to captain it, at his death. It is in the elaborate wall-paintings of the tombs of New Kingdom pharaohs in the Valley of the Kings that we find this concept most colourfully illustrated. From the end of Old Kingdom times onwards, a 'democratization' of beliefs occurred whereby the solar aspect of life after death became transferred to wider sections of the community, and eventually in late New Kingdom times to all and sundry. When everyone went to sail in the solar bark, the *cosmic* force of the myth which naturally applied to the king was diluted and the idea grew up that the dead sailed with the sun mainly on the nocturnal part of his journey through the underworld, returning to their tombs and preserved bodies during the day.

Also detectable towards the close of the Old Kingdom is yet another cycle of funerary beliefs which came to play a great part in ancient Egyptian thinking about the after-life. This is the complex of ideas associated with Osiris. Osiris, like others of the world's resurrection gods, may have had some muddled historical basis: in the Egyptian case, in the form of a king or series of kings who were ritually killed off and buried at some point in their reign in order to promote the yearly regeneration of the land. A whole mythology was subsequently elaborated about Osiris' murder by an evil brother, Seth, and the gathering together of the fragments of his mutilated body by his wife and sister, Isis, who managed to conceive a son by him 'posthumously', called Horus. What is clear is that Osiris was a god of renewal associated with the annual withering of the crops, corn in particular, and their annual restoration in springtime and with the annual rise and fall of the Nile. Osiris' concern with the death and rebirth of the natural vegetation and the sown crops of the Nile Valley naturally went hand in hand with his implication in the cycle of human birth and death. Tutankhamun's tomb contained, it may be recalled, a shallow tray figure of Osiris filled with mud from which corn stems had sprouted after the closure of the tomb. A papyrus in the Louvre depicts Osiris as a supine figure from which sprout stalks of corn and an erect phallus—a clear indication of the association of the ideas of renewal and resurrection with potency and fertility. Osiris came to attract to his mythology everything to do with death and resurrection, and was pictured ruling over the underworld; the dead aspired to occupation of a plot of land in Osiris' Kingdom where they could live again the life they had known in the Nile Valley. So Osiris' underworld came to resemble the Elysian Plain of the Greeks, and was called by the ancient Egyptians the 'Fields of Yalu'.

First for the royal dead only, but after Middle Kingdom times for all who could afford a decent burial at all, the custom grew up of identifying the deceased as the 'Osiris So-and-So', an expression that came eventually to have only the force of our 'the late So-and-So' formula. Osirian beliefs are probably involved in the bandaging of mummies: this bandaging may imitate the way in which Isis put back together the scattered fragments of the murdered Osiris' body; early mummies, like that of Nefer are padded, plastered and painted to look like the living rather than wrapped up in the classic fashion associated with all the New Kingdom and Late Period ones. With the passing of Egyptian greatness at the end of the New Kingdom, all the rich endowment in the way of elaborate tombs and grave-goods that had previously been lavished on the dead shrank down to a concern only with the mummy and its case. Latter-day mummies, in frequently very ugly coffins, have spells and magical texts written all over them in lieu of these discontinued riches.

The ancient Egyptians on the whole maintained an optimistic expectation of the after-life, in contrast as we have seen to some other ancient civilizations where drearier prospects loomed. In the demoralized days of the late New Kingdom, during the reigns of the declining Ramessides, a darker side of ancient Egyptian belief was developed in which guilt and judgment and fear of purgatorial experiences in the next world predominated, but that is not typical of the Egyptian spirit. Even so, the materialistic and over-concrete imagery of ancient Egyptian belief can easily summon up a rather crude impression of the nature of the Egyptian after-life. When all was said about the 'houses of eternity' and journeyings in the solar boat or easy living in the Fields of Yalu, the ancient Egyptians were at the same time capable of a deeper strain in their reflections upon the next world, as is disclosed in a scribe's instructional papyrus of Late Period times where a human soul seeks an answer to the problem of death from the great creator-god Atum:

Soul: O Atum, what does it mean that I must go into the wilderness (of death)? It has no water, it has no air, it is very deep, very dark and boundless.

Atum: You will live there without care in a land of silence.

Soul: But one cannot find there the satisfaction of love-making.

Atum: I have put blessedness in the place of water, air and love-making; and peace of mind in place of bread and beer.

This is a long way from the notions of sailing in the solar bark of the sun-god or working in Osiris' Elysian Fields; it is very far indeed from the simple expectation that the dead will go on inhabiting the familiar everyday world and enjoying the offerings of their relatives. The priesthoods of ancient Egypt did endeavour in New Kingdom and later times to syncretize the various religious cults that had come down to them from

Above *The average Egyptian looked forward to an after-life spent in the lush corn-fields of the underworld.*

Opposite page, top *Isis, the wife of Osiris, was the mother of Horus in the central holy family of ancient Egypt: she is often shown nursing the infant Horus.*
Centre *One aspect of the dead man's surviving spirit was pictured as a human-headed bird, the Ba.* Bottom *Osiris, pictured here in a papyrus illustration, was a god of resurrection, fertility and vegetative abundance.*

148

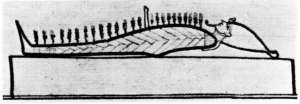

earlier days, and beliefs about the after-life were included in these attempts at comprehensive systems. The so-called 'Book of the Dead' belongs to these efforts. In reality, the phrase would be better translated as 'The Book of What is in the Underworld' and there is not one but several versions of this sort of work. Such books, in the form of papyrus rolls, were usually placed in the tombs of the richer dead from New Kingdom times, sometimes actually wound into the mummy-wrappings. They are not systematic works of theology or philosophy, but really catalogues of spells and magical formulae designed to help the deceased through the incidents of the next life. Probably they, or something like them, were read out by the priests who officiated at the burial. They include all the tricks of the trade necessary to gain passage in the sun-god's boat, to become identified with Osiris, to have the dead man admitted into the underworld, to enable him to defeat his enemies. They do not include much in the way of curses of the sort imputed to Tutankhamun by sensationalist newspapermen. Since so much of what we know about the Egyptians is owed to their funerary practices, and, since this situation has sometimes cast an unwarranted morbidity over the popular estimation of Egyptian civilization, it is worth closing this account of everyday life and life after death in ancient Egypt with the reminder that not only were no curses and no texts of any sort found in Tutankhamun's tomb but moreover the very idea of curses upon the living by the dead was never deeply ingrained in the Egyptian spirit. A truer picture of the Egyptian approach to life and to mortality comes from 'The Song of the Harper' that was first written up in the tomb of a Middle Kingdom king: 'All living things breathe the air, at the appointed time they give birth to their children, then they go to their tomb . . . there is no one who will not pass into the other world, life on earth is only as long as a dream . . . no one returns from the grave to tell us how they are . . . or to lighten our hearts until we too go there'. And so 'May one whom you love sit beside you. Let there be music and singing. Put care aside and think only of pleasure until the time comes for you to go to the land of silence'.

Chapter VIII The Technical and Scientific Achievements of Ancient Egypt

Science in the modern sense did not exist in ancient Egypt. What there was of scientific knowledge could not be disentangled as a separate entity from a total body of beliefs and attitudes that were far from scientific; and scientific method was severely limited by an everyday and rule-of-thumb approach to problems that discouraged generalization and theory.

Practical aptitudes of various sorts were certainly required of the Egyptians and were part and parcel of their successful exploitation of the Nile Valley. 'Geometry' is a compound of two Greek words and means land-measurement: it is obvious that at least practical geometry, if not geometrical theory, was of great importance to the Egyptians. Every year the rising Nile obliterated for a period the boundaries of fields and estates up and down the land and when the waters receded some sort of rapid surveying work was often required to re-establish the limits of the plots and holdings. The Egyptians employed more or less standardized units of length for their measurements and also possessed units of area for assessing the size and tax-potential of pieces of land-ownership. The reckoning of time and season was also important to them and the Egyptians elaborated a calendar which differed considerably from our own. The three seasons (of summer, inundation and winter) were made up of four months each and each month contained three weeks of ten days apiece. The division of time inside the individual day was achieved by means of water-clocks wherein water flowing out of a hole in a vessel gradually reduced its level by reference to a series of hour-marks inscribed inside. The Greeks took up this device as the 'clepsydra'. The Egyptians seem to have used a different set of marks at the different seasons so that the number of hours in the day remained constant throughout the year but the length of these hours in absolute terms varied.

Observation of the stars, particularly of the dog-star Sirius whose appearance heralded the inundation, played a large part in Egyptian life. Astronomical observations were also of geometric application, for the usually clear skies of Egypt made the stars a reliable guide to orientation on the ground. The so-called 'imperishable stars', by which the Egyptians meant the circumpolar bodies that never set and so never pass into the underworld of the dead, were almost certainly the key to accurate compass-point orientation. The famous precision of the alignment of the faces of some of the pyramids was no doubt owed to accurate observation of the polar region of the sky about which the rest of the stars rotate.

Profitable handling of the Nile also required considerable engineering skill: remember the achievement credited to the legendary first pharaon, Menes, in damming the Nile near Memphis and reclaiming land for building and agricultural purposes. Water-works of all kinds were a feature of ancient Egypt from the very earliest days and extensive canal-digging dates back at least as far as the Middle Kingdom. During that period, the Fayum Depression was the scene of massive irrigation under-takings that reclaimed large areas of land and regularized the Nile's access to the Fayum streams and lake by means of an artificial channel. At least by the time of queen Hatshepsut of the New Kingdom, who sent off her expedition to Punt along it, a partly artificial channel linking the Nile to the Red Sea was in operation. Boats, incidentally, and not bridges, were the means by which the Nile was crossed. Some were purely river boats: simple skiffs of resin-filled papyrus or acacia-wood vessels (cedar was used for royal boats), but ocean-going ships were also employed. There were early voyages on the Red Sea and the 'Great Green', or Mediter-ranean. If the papyrus boat was the simplest sort of craft (and there are parts of Africa where such boats are still in use—Thor Heyerdahl used two of them, in larger versions, to reach America), then the sort of huge ship buried alongside Cheops' Pyramid represents the sophisticated mode of ancient Egyptian ship-building. Constructed in cedar and equipped with a cabin and steering-oars, a boat like this serves to show the style in which the king was used to travel up and down his domain: it was probably buried alongside his pyramid (as happened in the case of other royal burials) as part of the complex of beliefs about the king's style of life in the next world where he would ride across the sky in the boat of the sun-god or sail on the waters of the underworld. Cedar was traditionally imported from Lebanon, where ocean-going boats were developed at an early stage. Once arrived in Egypt, the cedar wood was perhaps transported to Upper Egypt from the Delta ports by floating it on the Nile.

The Egyptian's use of the 'Nilometer' at Aswan to record and predict the inundation-levels of the Nile has already been noted—another of their technical innovations, which was illustrated in a New Kingdom tomb at Thebes, was the 'shaduf'. The shaduf (an Arabic word) is a simple but effective device using a counterweight to raise water from one level to another: examples identical with the ancient illustration can even be seen in use today in the Egyptian countryside, though the driven pump is

Above *A full-size Nile boat was buried in a pit alongside the pyramid of Cheops.*

Below left *A New Kingdom tomb shows the operation of a water-raising 'shaduf' identical to ones still in use in Egypt today.*

Below right *Metalworkers used to cast and cold-beat copper, bronze and precious metals in ancient Egypt.*

replacing them nowadays. The water wheel, turned by oxen, was not introduced until the Late Period, after the end of the New Kingdom.

The great days of ancient Egypt belong to the Bronze Age and even to the earlier copper-working phase—iron was very rare in Egypt until well after inhabitants of Anatolia, like the Hittites, had pioneered its use towards the end of the second millennium BC. An iron dagger was found in the Bronze Age tomb of Tutankhamun, but its very rarity was what probably made it a treasured possession of that young king. Until New Kingdom times, copper alone was the metal material of the ancient Egyptians—thereafter, a quantity of tin was usually mixed in to produce bronze. Copper was beaten cold and also melted and moulded. The melting process was known to the Egyptians as 'causing the metal to swim' and was conducted in a crucible over a fire that was encouraged by being blown upon through reeds. Later on, these reeds were piped into leather bellows-bags that were pumped by hand or foot in a manner exactly paralleled in parts of Africa today. Solid casting of such tools as axes, adzes, chisels, drills, saws and graving points was common, and in New Kingdom times large temple doors were cast solid in bronze. The 'lost-wax' technique was used as early as the Archaic Period to cast more complex forms: in this technique an intricate wax pattern of the item to be cast is fashioned up on a clay core and embedded in soft clay which follows all the details of the pattern; when the whole is fired the wax melts and is lost through channels in the clay, leaving a hard ceramic mould into which the melted copper or bronze can be poured to assume all the intricate shapes of the original pattern; when the mould is broken open (and so, incidentally, destroyed) a marvellously complex casting emerges in metal. A pair of Sixth Dynasty statues of king Phiops I and son combine beaten copper sheeting with details in the lost-wax technique. From the Late Period, mass-produced little bronzes of a votive nature are ten-a-penny at Sakkara near Memphis. Gold was cast, too, for more precious and significant pieces (gold-mining was a pharaonic prerogative like stone-quarrying). The gold falcon-head from Hieraconpolis ('Falcon-City') is a fine example of such work, as is the golden regalia of queen Aahotep and the fabulous portrait mummy-mask of Tutankhamun, beaten out of no more than two pieces of gold sheet. Perhaps the great solid gold inner coffin of Tutankhamun is the most amazing of all pieces of ancient Egyptian gold-working—certainly it transcends the showy vulgarity of much of Tutankhamun's grave goods. Gold could be obtained within the pharaoh's domains, but silver was harder to come by and was consequently expensive and rare until the Eighteenth Dynasty when imperial conquests made it cheaper and a bit more plentiful.

Of course, woodworking went on extensively throughout the Bronze Age and, thanks to the high preservation possibilities of the Egyptian scene, a great deal of wooden material has survived to us; Tutankhamun's tomb contained a lot of wooden objects, including many pieces of furniture, but fine wooden furniture also dates back to much earlier times: from the burial shaft of Hetepheres at Giza, near the pyramid of her son Cheops, come a canopy framework, a bed and a chest of great beauty and there is in the Manchester University Museum a well-preserved wooden bed of the Archaic Period. Woodworking, whether of furniture or ships or the tools that were employed in the construction of stone monuments, was always to the fore.

The management of their vast building enterprises has always fascinated students of the ancient Egyptians' technical achievements. The construction of the pyramids, above all, remains such an impressive accomplishment that some commentators have been led even in modern times to speculate whether these daunting works could only have been carried out with mysterious forces of which we know nothing today. Really the only force of which most of us nowadays know less than our ancestors is sheer back-breaking toil on a scale to compare with rock-breaking on Devil's Island! Traces of the techniques employed in Egyptian stone-quarrying have survived: at Aswan, the granite quarries from which great obelisks were cut still show lines of wedge-slots that the ancient workmen used in splitting rock. The method was to find a fault and exploit this line of weakness by cutting slots into the rock with still harder tools and then inserting wooden wedges which might swell up when wetted and so crack apart the faulty rock. Another method involved the building of low mud-brick walls along the fault lines (or any line where it was desired to cut the rock) to contain fires of brushwood that would rapidly heat up the rock before the sudden application of cold water caused splitting of the stone. Continual pounding with balls of hard dolorite was used to break up the rock treated by the fire-and-water method. In the Aswan quarries evidence of the removal of much stone is abundant and capped by the presence of a half-extracted obelisk still lying in the scene of operations. What seems to have happened here is that the New Kingdom quarriers, well on their way to carving out their biggest-ever obelisk, discovered a fault within the body of the projected monument. Almost certain breakage would have attended any attempt to get the whole thing out, ship it down to Thebes and erect it. So they gave it up and left it where it was. They were

The obelisk raft from reliefs in Hatshepsut's temple.

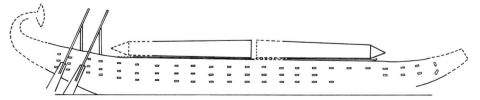

155

usually quite successful with these monuments as surviving examples at Thebes and Cairo (and now London, Paris, Rome and New York) illustrate. The sort of barges that were used to float off the extracted obelisks are illustrated in Hatshepsut's temple and along the causeway of king Wenis. While cedar from Lebanon was being towed up the Nile from the Delta, granite was being shipped down the river from Aswan in Upper Egypt. Erection of the unwieldly obelisks was almost certainly achieved by means of ramps of sand and mud-brick. Mud-bricks were made in Egypt, then as now, by mixing Nile mud with straw to re-inforce it and forming the mixture in simple wooden moulds: bricks without straw fell apart. The remains of ramps made of mud-brick have survived against the wall of one of the great pylon gates of the Karnak temple and they point to the method used in raising such structures. An obelisk would have been dragged foot-first to the top of a colossal ramp and then let down a steeper slope by ropes and possibly by the removal of a supporting body of sand until it stood upon its base. Very possibly the ramps would have been more impressive to our eyes than the monument left high-and-dry when they had been removed.

Certainly the ramps involved in pyramid-building must have been prodigious affairs. It has been claimed that traces of the foundations of such ramps, covering very great lengths of ground, have been noted at Giza. A ramp that led directly up to the face of a pyramid would have been a very difficult device to maintain, however, since it would have required constant increasing of its height and length (as the pyramid rose layer by layer) unless impossibly steep approach-angles were finally to be faced. Such a ramp would have enclosed a terrific volume of sand and dwarfed the pyramid itself, which is hard to believe in the case of the gigantic pyramids of Cheops and Chephren. Some students have suggested a system of four ramps running, not up to the faces of the pyramids at right angles, but along those faces and so involving a lot less sand and mud-brick and not becoming impossibly huge.

Up these ramps the blocks of the pyramid would have been hauled on wooden sledges or dragged over rollers. Both sledges and rollers are suggested by ancient Egyptian reliefs depicting the transport of monuments of various sorts. The wheel was not employed at this time. Perhaps a counterweight device rather like the shaduf, only for stones instead of water, was employed as well. Certainly the pulley, any more than the wheel until New Kingdom times, was not a mechanical device used by the ancient Egyptians, but a stone-raising version of the shaduf's pivot and beam is a possibility, and no doubt long levers were also employed to move the blocks. There is no reason to doubt that such simple devices as ramps and rollers and levers, given a large and dedicated (or adequately coerced) labour force and a decade or so to labour in, could have achieved the building of the pyramids. The impressive degree of precision achieved in some of the structures of ancient Egypt is owed to painstaking employment of stellar-orientation, plumb-lines, lines of sight and water-levels. The laying out of the base-area of the pyramids would have been accomplished by means of trenches of water to find levels and observation of the polar region of the sky to arrive at accurate compass orientation, together with sighting along lines of markers and plumb determinations of the vertical. Even the complex interior construction of the Great Pyramid could have been achieved by refinements of these simple techniques.

If the technical and engineering accomplishments of the Egyptians continue to impress us, we must face the fact that these feats were achieved on the basis of a supremely practical approach to the problems involved and to all intents and purposes without the help of any sort of scientific theorizing. The Greeks supposed that they themselves had derived the foundations of their sciences from the Egyptians but really the Egyptians were lacking in the spirit of generalization and theory, to say nothing of the experimental method, that we should regard as scientific. Of course the classical Greeks were not scientists either in the modern sense, and medically speaking for instance the Egyptians sometimes had the drop on them—it is unlikely that an Egyptian, used to everyday practicalities, could have declared as Aristotle did without looking further into the matter that women had a different number of teeth from men.

Egyptian medicine, as it has survived to us in some papyrus texts, is a mixture of quite careful observation and sensible treatments with frankly magical elements. Doctors were quite often the priests of Sekhmet, the lioness-headed goddess of epidemics. The duality of baneful and healing qualities inherent in this deity made her an ideal patroness of the medical men. One medical papyrus shows these doctors and surgeons to have been capable of detailed diagnoses of symptoms and plausible prognoses as to the likelihood of recovery. There were apparently three categories of patient—the favourable, the doubtful and the hopeless. Treatment could be rational enough, with dietary prescriptions (like honey for coughs) and recommendations of rest. For severer cases, which time alone would not heal, there was resort to manipulation and surgery. But it has to be said that, for a people habituated to poking into bodies and removing organs in the course of mummification, the Egyptians possessed no great anatomical knowledge and surgical skill with the living. The anatomical pioneers of our own era had to have recourse to Burke and Hare and other 'resurrection men' to gather the sort of data that the Egyptians could have easily acquired. Perhaps mummification was too sacred a proceeding for experimental medicine to intrude. There was a distinction, moreover, between injury and medical misadventure whose treatment was approached on a rational basis, and diseases like infections or cancer whose origins could not be fathomed and which were put down to the interventions of the gods or of the dead and 'treated' with magical means. On the everyday

157

level of conditions that could be understood and handled in a practical fashion, the Egyptians acquitted themselves reasonably well: bones were set with some success, mechanical methods of contraception were devised, useful plants were employed as drugs and castor oil was known and applied; on the other hand a misguided and dangerous emphasis was put on the use of animal droppings that strikes us as unreasonable.

As well as a flair for the use of herbal medicines, the Egyptians were credited with a considerable knowledge of chemistry by other peoples of the ancient world. Indeed, the very word for the semi-magical pursuit out of which the modern science of chemistry was born, 'Alchemy', is probably derived, via Arabic, from 'Kemet', 'the Black Land', Egypt. A striking instance of the Egyptians' occasional accomplishments in this field is seen in the so-called 'Egyptian faïence', a vivid blue-green glazing in the form of a covering of very siliceous glass over a quartz core. There are a great many beautiful objects from Egypt manufactured in this 'faïence' technique, like the New Kingdom hippopotamus in the British Museum.

A number of mathematical texts have survived from ancient Egypt and we possess seven in all on the basis of which to arrive at an estimation of the mathematical abilities of the Egyptians. As might be expected the ancient Egyptians made no attempt to elucidate the properties of numbers or arrive at a general theory of mathematics (as is involved in the modern study and to some extent in that of the Greeks); rather they wielded a system based on experience and reached by a process of trial and error. Laying out foundations in two dimensions and building up structures in three, on the basis of quite simple fixed proportions like the right-angled three-four-five triangle, allowed them to derive in a concrete manner from the actual results of their labours new values and relationships of measurements that were not foreseen when work began. These newly appreciated values could then be applied to new works, and all this process could be advanced without any theory whatsoever but by the simple accumulation of observations.

The metrication of the Egyptians was for the most part decimal in principle for measurements of distance, area and capacity. Their week was made up of ten days. The decimal principle made for easy multiplication and division by ten, and of course doubling and halving were also easy manoeuvres. Series of halvings and doublings, with the addition of single units, were the basis of multiplication and division by factors other than ten and two. There was no zero (an invention of the medieval Arab mathematicians) but the concept was foreshadowed in the occasional leaving of spaces for it. To π was assigned the value of 3·16, which was not a bad approximation for the time.

Among the technical achievements of ancient Egypt must be counted their development of writing. Whether or not the idea of writing was adopted from an outside source, perhaps from the Sumerians whose

158

At Karnak, behind one of the pylon-gates, a mud-brick ramp used in its construction nearly three thousand years ago was never removed at the end of the work.

earliest known writing does pre-date Egyptian examples, the Egyptians certainly developed a highly idiosyncratic system of their own (which is, co-incidentally, the most beautiful form of writing ever developed—at least in its classical hieroglyphic form). The longhand hieratic and demotic versions were, of course, ultimately based upon the hieroglyphs, but were better adapted for rapid use on papyrus, wood or leather. Champollion discovered that the hieroglyphs were a method of writing down the precise meaning of a real language, rather than magical signs. He was able to translate them with the aid of his knowledge of Coptic and to begin to recognize some of the terrific complexities of the system.

Briefly, what faces us in the hieroglyphic writing is a mixture of ideogram and phonogram: in other words, the system is neither purely a representational one (where pictures of things mean simply the things they show) nor an alphabetic one (where the sounds of words are objectively spelled out by signs with strict sound values). Presumably an ideographic phase lies at the beginning of all writing systems, but even in Sumer the existence of a purely ideogram period has been disputed. In Egypt, apart from a few very early instances where a single sign (like the scorpion on the late pre-dynastic mace-head) serves to stand in for a whole piece of meaning, and even then it is not really an ideogram simply depicting the thing it shows, there is an ideogram-plus-phonogram system from the first. This mixture continued till the very end, when Greek letters were adopted to write the Coptic tongue. So it happens that a single sentence may contain lone signs, like a stylized drawing of a house, that stand for the thing they depict, as well as groups of signs that simply spell out a word, like the bolt of cloth, the swallow and the mouth that make up s w r, 'to drink'. It is obvious that while concrete objects and some verbs might be handled purely ideographically, complex abstractions and grammatical features like the tenses and moods of verbs would be very hard to render in that way. The step between ideogram and phonogram seems to have come about because some words, like the word for 'house', had the same sound as another word with a different meaning—in this case, the verb 'to go out'—so their sign could mean both words according to context. Context was sometimes helped along by the use of determinatives which were sense signs that indicated the general area of meaning: a walking man hieroglyph would distinguish 'go out' from 'house'. The next stage was simply to regard the sound of a given sign as a component in building up the sound of a longer word with a different meaning altogether— so the swallow sign could mean just w r wherever that combination was required. Of course, these hypothetical phases of development are not in evidence archaeologically: the fully developed system was in use in the earliest texts that have come down to us.

The Egyptians' image of their environment and the relationships between the various parts of it—in other words, their knowledge of geography—was rather sketchy. But, in keeping with their practical

Above *In the late temple of Dendera a star-map since called a zodiac, was carved.*

Below *The Egyptians developed a chemical technique for producing a sort of glazed quartz called 'Egyptian faïence', here applied to a small hippopotamus.*

161

Above *The prodigious feats of the Egyptians in shipping their obelisks on the Nile were eclipsed by the nineteenth century engineers who floated some of them back to Europe.*

Above *At the base of this obelisk queen Hatshepsut recorded the details of its cutting and erection.*

Left *The unfinished obelisk in the quarries at Aswan was abandoned when threatening faults were discovered in the stone.*

natures, they were able to formulate a useful picture of where their friends and enemies lived and how to get there. Their own land was geographically straightforward in that the river flowed down from top to bottom (the Egyptian faced south when considering his own geography) and the sun crossed roughly at a right angle to the river from east to west. More precise orientation was afforded by the circumpolar stars which could be observed by means of looking along two fixed markers or maybe up the narrow entrance corridor of a pyramid (pyramids usually had entrances in their northern faces). The star that moved least of all in relation to painstakingly aligned points was close to the very pole itself—of course, as a result of the precession of the equinoxes (the earth's wobbling on its axis as it rotates and circles the sun) the pole-star at various points in Egyptian history was not the north star of today. The Egyptians were not aware that a rotating spheroid planet created the observed movement of the stars around the pole—indeed they thought that the earth was flat, picturing it as an expanse of land with the Nile running down the middle and with sea all round. Four pillars were thought to support the sky at the corners and beneath the land washed the waters of the underworld, or possibly there existed an inverted replica for the dead of the living land above.

The Egyptians knew where to go to find their foreign neighbours but they had no clear idea where those foreign lands lay in relation to themselves. Just as a visitor to London may be able to reach Piccadilly Circus by tube without having much idea where this place objectively resides, so the Egyptians knew how to cross the desert to the Red Sea and sail to Punt or march through Sinai to Palestine and the river Orontes without relating these places together as a man with a modern map might do. The pharaoh Necho of the Twenty-sixth Dynasty who concerned himself with the canal to the Red Sea also wanted to know whether Libya (by which he understood all of Africa to the west of Egypt) had sea around it and he dispatched a crew of Phoenician sailors to find out for him the hard way. These Phoenicians sailed down the Red Sea and then on down the coast of Africa, round the Cape and up the west African coast into the Mediterranean through the straits of Gibraltar and back to the Egyptian Delta. The voyage took them three years and they experienced during part of it what was for them the exciting situation of being to the west of a sunrise that came up on their landward side. On the Red Sea and in Punt the sun always came up over sea with land to the west and now here came a sunrise from the landward side. 'Libya' was indeed surrounded by sea. The fact that Necho should have seen fit to finance this expedition confirms that the Egyptians' knowledge of geography was limited to their own country and a few glimpses of their near neighbours.

Since the Egyptians have been frequently credited with a depth of knowledge and technical expertise quite beyond their actual attainments, it is worth emphasizing once again that everything we know about them reveals them to have been an unusually untheoretical civilization with a cheerful lack of concern for everything that has characterized philosophic inquiry since the ancient Greeks. Where down-to-earth and everyday methods would suit, they were content to employ them and even when they went beyond the world of ordinary experience, their very flights of fancy— like those concerning life after death—have a materialistic ring to them. Their latter-day reputation for all things occult is a serious misunderstanding of their real attitudes. An instance of the extent to which they have been misunderstood is provided by what we know about their astronomical work. The ancient Egyptians, at least until very late days when they came under the influence of some Mesopotamian and Persian ideas, had no notion of astrology. They did observe the heavens, identify constellations and note the motions of the stars, but they did not elaborate any ideas of astrological influences upon the affairs of men and they did not cast horoscopes. What have been described as zodiacs like the 'Zodiac' of Dendera, are in fact star maps (however inaccurate) grouped according to the Egyptian constellations. In fact, the Egyptians based their constellations upon the patterns of the Babylonians, who were more practised star-gazers than the Egyptians themselves, whereas our own are derived from the fancies of the Greeks.

Finally to dispel any lingering suspicion that the ancient Egyptians may have been somehow endowed with a technical expertise or body of scientific knowledge that has altogether escaped us nowadays, we may note that among the texts that have survived there are examples of formal problems that the scribes set for each other, rather like the schoolbook exercises of today, where challenges are thrown out to calculate the number of men needed to shift huge monuments of specified sizes or to devise means for putting such monuments exactly where they were wanted. The ancient Egyptians, moreover, sometimes made mistakes and failed to bring off some piece of work—such is the case with one of Hatshepsut's great obelisks in the Karnak temple, which has been erected markedly out of square, missing the groove cut to orientate it. On the same monument, Hatshepsut has had inscribed in the most matter-of-fact way that this obelisk and its twin nearby 'are made from a single block of hard granite, without any patching. I ordered work on them from the first day of Winter of year fifteen (of my reign), until the last day of Summer of year sixteen, making seven months of work in the quarry'.

Chapter IX The Egyptian Outlook

The great technical expertise and sheer perseverance of the Egyptians in engineering matters did not become the basis of a scientific world-view. It remained for the ancient Greeks to create the idea of Science, with a capital S, as distinguished from piety. The Ionian philosophers who took the first steps towards establishing the natural sciences were sceptical men living in free-spirited commercial communities, quite unlike ancient Egyptian society where even the most learned and gifted thinkers were unlikely to want to inquire into the workings of the universe in an experimental and open-minded spirit. It simply would not have occurred to them to do so, since the entire outlook upon life that they had absorbed with their mothers' milk centred upon the idea of a god-given cosmos, continuously renewed by the divine powers and managed by a living god, which called for no further explanation, let alone justification. Unlike those pioneering Greeks, the Egyptian thinkers inhabited (in happy times at least) a complex, stable and self-sufficient social scene, permeated with theological attitudes and undisturbed by commercial or democratic values. Their view of life left no room for, and did not need, scientific thought.

The Egyptians sought, none the less, to equip themselves with some sort of account of the world and its workings—'explanation' is a modern concept which would not quite fit the Egyptian approach. Cosmology is a well-worked scientific study in our time, offering hypotheses about the way the universe functions and what its origins, if any, may have been. The Egyptians, without benefit of physics, supplied themselves with a series of images of creation which set out to describe the way in which the whole world had come into existence; but these visions were not reached by a process of scientific observation and experiment, rather they were developed in accordance with the particular psychological flavour of the Egyptian view of the world.

The Egyptians saw no need for a single creation story any more than they maintained a single view of the after-life. There are several accounts of how the world came into being, associated with different cultural centres, but it would be a mistake to think that people in one place believed one thing and people in another place another—the Egyptians welcomed the richness of insights that different visions could simultaneously provide. One must shed the western prejudice, both scientific and pre-scientific, that monolithic explanation alone will suffice to make life comprehensible.

The prototype image lying behind all Egyptian creation-myths was supplied by the Nile Valley itself. The annual death in inundation and re-birth of the land of Egypt is the common thread in all the Egyptian cosmo-gonies. Each year, as the waters of the flooding Nile receded, narrow bars of land along the banks of the winter stream re-emerged from the depths, ready and fertile for sowing with seed. And so, the Egyptian creation stories share the basic concept that out of the passive waters of chaos there arose in the first place a primeval mound of earth. The waters of the primordial ocean continued to encircle the world and to gush forth from the cataracts as an image of the source of the Nile, but the land that had arisen out of these waters at 'the First Time' marked the creation of the earth. Two main examples of the way in which the Egyptians handled this basic material were developed in Heliopolis and Memphis, both close to present-day Cairo.

In the Heliopolitan version the primeval mound rises out of the waters with a pyramid-shaped stone upon it, at the tip of which the creator-god Atum manifests himself. Sometimes the 'phoenix', actually a species of heron, was pictured as the image of this divine epiphany. Atum created the rest of the gods by means of his spittle or semen—in other words, out of himself acting alone. The first pair he so created gave birth to the rest by mating, and among the gods brought into being in this way were Isis and Osiris, about whom another cycle of myths was woven. Atum was identified with the sun-god Re as Re-Atum, uniting the roles of first creator and perpetual upholder of the universe. Re was simultaneously associated with Horus, the ancient falcon-imaged sky-god, as Re-Horakhty. In the person of the king, these images came together with the Osiris myth, for the living ruler of Egypt was considered to be both 'the son of Re' and the living Horus, avenging son of his father Osiris who ruled in the world of the dead.

At Memphis, the creation story centred upon the great god of that city, Ptah. Ptah was called 'the Risen Earth' and directly identified with the primeval mound. He was, among other things, the patron god of crafts-manship and it is interesting to recall that his city of Memphis was tradi-tionally founded by the first pharaoh, Menes, who reclaimed its land from the waters of the Nile. Like Atum at Heliopolis, Ptah of Memphis con-tained the whole world within himself: the raw material of the living earth,

166

Above *Some little wooden objects from the Egyptian tombs are lighthearted studies of everyday life, like this swimming girl that formed the handle of a cosmetic spoon.*

Left *A satirical papyrus picture demonstrates the extreme antiquity of the 'Tom and Jerry' theme.*

Below *Ptah was one of the creator-gods: what his mind thought up his tongue uttered and thereby brought into existence.*

Below *The phoenix, actually a sort of heron, was supposed to appear on the top of a pillar at the creation of the world.*

167

its stones and soil and vegetation, its animals and men, its gods. All things were the expression of Ptah's thought and word—he made the world by 'thinking it up' and uttering it. As a late theological treatise (tantalizingly inscribed on a block that has since been partly defaced by use as a mill-stone) puts it: 'it is the tongue which utters what has been thought by the heart'. The rest of the gods, in this version, were aspects of Ptah identified with his various organs: thus ibis-headed Thoth, the scribe and messenger of the gods, was Ptah's tongue. In the same way, Re too declares: 'I am a god with many names and many forms and my form is in every god'. From these instances, it seems clear that a sort of 'monotheistic' vision of divinity was always present in ancient Egypt, but at the same time the Egyptians were not content to limit the expression of deity to a single jealous God. Egyptian texts, indeed, frequently allude to 'God' in a singular and generalized fashion that makes it possible for us to approach many of their religious ideas without the distractions of their vivid and various renderings of their many individual deities. The world that the creator-god (whether seen as Atum or Ptah or whatever) had made was not the world that western man has been intellectually habituated to live in. The Greek philosophers, the Christian tradition and much of scientific thought have conspired to leave us with a prejudice in favour of singular purpose and one-way direction in life. For the Christian individual, life has been presented as a progression from birth through this world into death and transfiguration with no looking back; the Christian version of history fixes upon a single, unique and irredeemably significant event, changing the world for ever. Scientific thought has been dominated for over a hundred years by the notion of evolution which has quite properly been extended from relevance only to biology and is currently applied to awe-inspiring speculations about the ever-changing evolution of galaxies and whole universes over tens of billions of years. The social experience of the modern world has rubbed in the message that all things must change and has found scientific expression in the theories of Marxism, which share with Darwinism the concept of a natural progression of forms. The general proposition of unavoidable change was heralded by Shakespeare at the beginning of the modern age:

> When I have seen such interchange of state,
> Or state itself confounded to decay;
> Ruin hath taught me thus to ruminate,
> That Time will come and take my love away.

Whether expressed with gloomy courage, as in the poet's case, or optimistically by the Christian or Marxist, or neutrally (on the face of it) by the scientist—this idea of change and progression has had a firm grip upon almost all of western thought. The ancient Egyptians simply did not regard the world in this way.

The difference of the Egyptian view can best be gauged from their art; in particular, as expressed in sculpture, painting and architecture. Obviously, Egyptian art in the fields of music and dance has all but vanished (though friezes of dancers survive) and it must be said that Egyptian literature—while it offers examples of short stories and love-poems among its other forms—is not in terms of art on a par with western literature since Homer. If we understand by Egyptian art the realms of architecture, painting and sculpture, then we are faced at once with work of unmistakable excellence which does not accord with our traditional ideas of what great art must be. Ideas of evolution have been misapplied in this respect: in keeping with a sort of crude Darwinism, what comes later has seemed to be of necessity better, so Greek art has frequently been compared with Egyptian art greatly to the detriment of the latter, as though Egyptian art had not a different intent but had simply failed to match up to the aims of the Greeks. Greek art, for one thing, is full of a tension and striving (frequently with an erotic basis) that did not interest the Egyptians, since they wanted to reveal another sort of state of being.

When Egyptian art first arrived in quantity in Europe, in the age of looting, pieces often appeared without provenance and usually without any idea of their age or relationship with other examples of the same art. Museums filled up with statues and fragments of wall-paintings whose lack of any chronological ordering or known site of origin made it very easy for them to be regarded as an undistinguished whole, with very generalized traits. This undoubtedly accounts for much of the reputation of monotony and timelessness that Egyptian art still enjoys. When pieces from the Old Kingdom were taken indiscriminately along with Ptolemaic examples, when no one knew to what period Egyptian remains belonged, it was all too simple to lump them together and regard Egyptian art, as Winckelmann did, as 'a great desert plain which can be dominated from the tops of two or three high towers'. In fact, Egyptian art knew its periods like any other developing form and changed in accordance with the changing course of Egyptian history.

If Egyptian art has been unfavourably compared with Greek art, it has also been patronized for its failure to resemble photography and Victorian town-hall statuary. It is a commonplace to say that in Egyptian paintings and relief carvings legs are shown sideways-on while torsos grow upwards to a frontal view, that heads are shown in profile but eyes as though seen from the front. True, these features do not resemble the results of photography, but then the Egyptians were out to portray a quality that most photography cannot reveal. When photography arrived in the nineteenth century, a critic was led to assert that 'from today, painting is dead'. The sort of painting he had in mind was the whole tradition of representational (and impressionistic) work that ran back in academic hands to the Renaissance re-discovery of Greek art. Egyptian art did not set out to represent in terms of 'true' perspective the look of the world, above all not the look of the *moment* (which most photography emphasizes), but to render the essentials of the scene according to the Egyptian view of life. It is worth remembering that representational perspectivism is only a particular sort of distortion of the world after all, and that so-called primitive peoples sometimes cannot recognize their world in photographs. To the Egyptians, representational art would certainly have looked like distortion—since it would have left out or insufficiently emphasized details that were important to them. By contrast with modern secular art or art created for patrons, Egyptian art had a religious function like ice age cave paintings or the tribal art of Africa. 'Art for art's sake' would have been as meaningless for the Egyptians as the concept of objective science. Their art—at least what has survived—was, moreover, largely mortuary in purpose, and focused mainly upon pharaoh. Its religious function was to regularize and essentialize the expression of eternity. That is not quite the same thing as 'timelessness', the quality most often attributed to Egyptian art, for the Egyptian artists wrestled continually with the problem of reconciling the particularity of a given study with the need for expression in terms of eternity, and the products of their struggles are sometimes outstanding works which reveal the transient individuality of the subject in an everlasting spirit. Though much of Egyptian art was made for the tomb, it does not morbidly record the mortality of its subjects nor fix its eyes upon their transfiguration in the next world as Christian funerary art has done, rather it celebrates this world and what is typical of life on earth. It makes no difference whether this very world or one supremely like it after death is concerned: the view of the after-life afforded by the wall-art of the Egyptian tombs is firmly based upon experience in this world, writ large.

What appealed to the ancient Egyptians was what recurs in life, not what happens only once. The recurrent is the eternal, the single event passes away. In the tombs of the dead, therefore, it was the function of this religious art to eternalize the typical and recurring aspects of life, like sowing and reaping, hunting and feasting; the same art, when applied to the statues of the gods in their temples, sought to give eternal expression to those divine qualities that never change and act forever in the world. Both applications of this art, in temple and tomb, could not help but celebrate the real world from which its examples were drawn. Nietzsche's Zarathustra, in a rare instance in the modern world, expresses something of the same feeling about life: 'Joy, however, does not want heirs, or children —joy wants itself, wants eternity, wants recurrence, wants everything eternally the same'.

It is only right to emphasize that, as with all the artistic products of past times, the current critic is bound to theorize on the basis of what has survived. We must face the fact of the loss of much purely secular art in

Below *The chaotic design of the prehistoric 'Oxford' Palette is not in keeping with the orderliness of most Egyptian art. Fifteen hundred years later, order and chaos were brought together on a coffer of Tutankhamun (above): behind the king order reigns; he fires into chaos.*

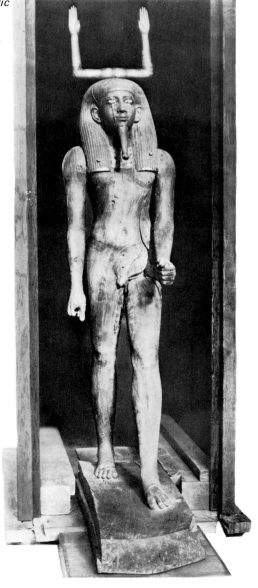

Right *A wooden statue of king Hor carries the 'Ka' sign on its head.*

Egypt: art that was not created for some everlasting purpose in temple or tomb, that was applied to the perishable homes of the living and has only haphazardly come down to us. There are tantalizing fragments of wall-paintings from ruined palaces and houses, there are traces of floor decoration at Akhenaten's Amarna, and these serve to show that a quite secular decorative art did exist in ancient Egypt, no doubt at all times. There are stray finds of 'toys', like the mechanical dwarfs operated on a pull-string, from a Middle Kingdom site and now in the Metropolitan Museum in New York and in the Cairo Museum; there are the lively sketches done upon fragments of pot or stone, called ostraca, which may in some cases be preliminary drafts for secular decorations—a lot of them were found by the craftsmen's tombs of Deir el-Medina at Thebes, and perhaps represent something of the non-funerary output of these artists. A well-known sketch from this site shows a fox and goat and another celebrated ostracon, now in the Turin Museum, depicts a female acrobat turning a somersault. Some of the ostraca, and some papyri—especially of late New Kingdom times, when social problems were to the fore—are of a satirical nature, showing a topsy-turvy world where, for example, mice are masters and cats servants. These little works run counter to the grand concerns of Egyptian religious art in as refreshing a way as the gargoyles and vignettes in medieval cathedrals. Another light-hearted aspect of Egyptian art is seen in the carved wooden cosmetic spoons whose handles often feature delightful carvings of flowers and, in particular, girls—like the swimming girl on one from Cairo. The signs are that a considerable amount of Egyptian art was, in fact, executed in wood, whose survival has not of course been nearly so sure as stone. Wooden funerary art exists from Old Kingdom times, where it perhaps belonged rather to the tombs of officials than to those of kings, whose statues were carved in stone, or occasionally cast and beaten in copper. From Middle Kingdom times comes a wooden statue of a king, the Ka-statue of king Hor.

The hieroglyphs themselves in a way set the style for all Egyptian art, with their concentration upon graphic essentials, their economy of expressiveness and their very concrete and direct imagery. The hieroglyphic system dates back to the earliest days of Egyptian history and its roots lie in predynastic times: predynastic art, as found upon pots and palettes and in the form of clay and ivory figurines, is of a markedly stylized character although it deals with human and animal figures and boats. Traces of Sumerian influence have been detected in some of the late predynastic pieces from Egypt, in particular on the knife handle from Jebel el-Arak which seems to show a Mesopotamian sort of hero-figure (bearded and hatted in an un-Egyptian way) and some boats of a Tigris-Euphrates pattern above more typically Egyptian examples. However that may be, there is no doubt that the characteristically Egyptian forms soon developed and are to be seen rapidly reaching maturity on the palettes of the

Previous page *At Amarna, the capital city of the heretic-pharaoh Akhenaten, more secular art has survived than is usual in ancient Egypt (because the city was abandoned and not repeatedly rebuilt), and this art is characterized by the nature-themes, handled realistically, that are a hall-mark of Akhenaten's style.*

Sketches and even developed little studies were often made on fragments of pottery or stone: their subject matter, as in the case of this girl acrobat, was frequently more secular and everyday than the themes of most surviving Egyptian art.

174

immediately Predynastic Period. The transition from a chaotic organization of the details (a Sumerian trait?), seen on the Oxford Palette, to the typically Egyptian ordering of the design in formal registers is revealed upon the Narmer Palette. The theme of chaos was employed again, much later in Egyptian history, during imperial involvement with Asia, upon the painted wooden coffer of Tutankhamun where register and disorder meet, and upon a giant face of the mortuary temple of Ramesses II where —around the dominating figure of the king—disorder reigns at the battle of Kadesh.

The Narmer Palette, already so important for historical reasons, is a key piece in tracing the early development of Egyptian art: here, at the beginning, the traits of simplification, of graphic concentration upon essentials, of the defusing of the tensions of a single transient event are well established. It is a great ideogram that expresses an aspect of the role of pharaoh: it does not so much record the occurrence of a single historical happening as celebrate the recurring pattern of the king's power to smash his enemies inside and outside Egypt. Narmer already rules on a symbolic plane, his striding pose is not a piece of action but a device to reveal the full essence of the king, his two strong legs and torso. The pseudo-stride is a common feature of Egyptian art, both painting and standing statuary (after all, statues are sometimes seen from the side), and serves well—as a photograph might not—to bring out the completeness of the person depicted. Some gods, like Ptah and Osiris, do not stride, for their nature does not require this sort of portrayal. The stride expresses in an essential and perfected way, as does the arm raised in symbolic smiting, the king's recurring and eternal role in meeting and subduing the enemies of his people: this is art *in the perfect tense*, showing not that some event once occurred but that a state has been achieved which embraces the accomplishment of the event for ever. It is clear that the aims of such art are quite different from those of Greek art and the mainstream of western art since the Renaissance; although the beginnings of Greek art may owe much to the Egyptian example, the Greeks soon elaborated their own genius in quite a different direction. When Egypt fell to the Greeks, grotesque attempts were sometimes made to put Greek heads on Egyptian bodies and the results are quite disturbing. Egyptian art must equally be contrasted with the Mesopotamian products: although Egyptian art pursues different aims from Greek art, it none the less remains—in its treatment of men and women—universal and humanistic in character while the art of the Sumerians and their successors is apt to look quite 'ethnographic' by comparison.

Not a great deal of art survives from the Archaic Period in Egypt, though one little ivory figure of a king from Abydos, now in the British Museum, his hunched shoulders wrapped around with a cloak, looks forward to the major statue of king Djoser that comes from his Third Dynasty

Above *Among the oldest wall-paintings from Egypt are these vividly pictured geese from Meidum.*

Above *The figure of Mycerinus displays a particular and idiosyncratic approach to portraiture towards the end of the Fourth Dynasty.*

Left *An unidentified early king of Egypt wears a long enveloping cloak as he walks forward in this little ivory figurine from Abydos.*

tomb enclosure at Sakkara. Like so much else in the Step Pyramid complex, this statue of Djoser represents a break-through and a grand beginning. It is the first life-size stone statue in the round from Egypt. It was found in the little chamber that butts on to the north face of the pyramid and, while the original is now in the Cairo Museum, a copy has been placed in the 'booth' to convey the impression of the intended design. The statue, which looks out from behind two small eye-holes, was meant to stand in for the person of the king in receiving offerings at his tomb. Djoser here wears a cloak over his rather hunched shoulders in the manner of the Abydos figurine. His face is damaged, no doubt at the hands of robbers of old who were after his inset eyes of some precious stone but even so its sombre severity is plain. His seated form has an almost emaciated look, with thin limbs, and strictly compares with the figure of Hesi-re (an official of the Third Dynasty) carved in relief on wooden panels from his tomb. These are both images of the living dead, conveying for ever the idea that an Egyptian might die and yet endure. Where Hesi-re's mien is neutral, as befits an official, king Djoser's expression is of royal power, emphasizing his cosmic role in overseeing Egypt in death as well as in life. In accordance with the potential and need of a complex and wealthy state (which Egypt in the Third Dynasty had clearly become) the concept of divine kingship inherited from earlier days—it survived in Africa till very recent times—has here been graced with a fresh artistic grandeur. In the underground passages beneath the Djoser pyramid and his south mastaba token-tomb, panels decorated with blue-green faïence tiles (representing the reed wall coverings of the palace of the living Djoser) carry depictions of the king performing various rituals to do with his role in life: he is seen frozen in the act of ritually running round his domain, for example.

Obviously these deeds carried an eternal significance and were rendered eternal in the carvings in his tomb. Although the king here is shown in vigorous guise, his close facial resemblance to the emaciated seated statue of Djoser is unmistakable. We are faced with a real portrayal of an individual man who happens at the same time to be a divine ruler with a cosmic role. The paradox of attempting to unite the portrait of a particular human being with the cosmic role of pharaoh runs through all Egyptian pharaonic art: the individual who occurs only once on earth must be depicted as the living god who recurs for ever. Egyptian artists enjoyed a varying success with this paradox and in any case the social role of pharaoh changed with time as Egyptian society progressed. In keeping with the religious nature of the art they produced, the Egyptian artists remained almost invariably anonymous: team-work without mention of individual leading-lights was the rule, though these masters undoubtedly existed and we can sometimes identify their finishing touches in wall-paintings and carvings. At Amarna we even know the name of the sculptor in whose workshop some famous pieces were found, but not because he signed any of them: these were not the narcissistic talents encountered in the bourgeois art world. The exception that proves this rule occurs on the statue of Djoser: the shoulder bears the name of Imhotep, architect of the whole complex, but this 'signature' did not set a style for his successors; at the most, the ancient artists sometimes slipped in a little picture of themselves on a tomb frieze, quietly observing all.　　　　　 —

From the Fourth Dynasty comes a series of statues, both of nobles and kings, that develops the paradox of the union of the transient with the eternal. The oldest piece of Egyptian wall-painting also comes from this dynasty, the geese from a tomb at Meidum, and the statue pair of prince Rahotep and his wife are painted in a vivid and life-like way that has survived astonishingly well. Although Rahotep is posed in much the same way as Djoser's statue, he has not the gaunt appearance of the living dead but a very vital fullness, like his wife. Living they may be, but they are all the same immobilized in an eternal posture, another instance of an achieved essential state, very much in the perfect tense. Other studies from this period display extremely individualistic traits, like the realistic bust of the middle-aged prince Ankhhaf: these are not the stylized-to-death portrayals often thought to constitute Egyptian art. No statue of Cheops or part thereof is currently available for study, but of his successor Chephren a remarkable life-size statue has come down to us. It is one of several that once stood in his valley temple at Giza, found toppled down a shaft in the course of excavation. Here is the figure of a strong, vital, living ruler, recognizable as an individual but idealized: the royal and divine version of Rahotep and wife. Where Djoser's extended arm lay, with palm flat on his thin thigh, Chephren's fist is clenched upon his vigorous limb. Chephren in his mortuary monument remains altogether a living force, and a particularized one in the form of an identifiable man, but seen from the point of view of his cosmic role, and very majestic. In fact, Chephren's majesty is all the clearer-cut if we compare him with the statues of his immediate successor Mycerinus, which edge towards an anecdotal and all-too-human portrayal with fleshy face and bulbous nose. In this case, the paradoxical union of the transient and individual with the everlasting and universal has fallen out rather badly. The retained formality of the pose consorts ill with the everyday humanity of the portrait.

In the Fifth Dynasty, the realism foreshadowed in the bust of Ankhhaf found full expression, at least in the non-royal pieces that have survived: above all in the wooden statue of Ka-aper, the so-called 'Village Headman' (because the Egyptian workmen on the excavation saw in him a likeness to their local sheik), where metaphysics have receded a very long way. At this time, the cult of the sun-god Re was very much in evidence: the rather badly built pyramids of the day were equipped with more elaborate

Above *At the end of the Old Kingdom, the nobles achieved a high degree of independence and self-aggrandisement, exemplified in this statue of Mereruka striding through his false door.*

Previous page *In the underground galleries of Djoser's Step Pyramid complex, a relief shows the king running around his domain in celebratory renewal of his reign.*

180

temples than before, of a sunnier and more nature-centred sort with columns carved as lotus, papyrus and palm; in the sun-sanctuary of Niuserre at Abusir, an obelisk stood on a platform in an open court and the passage leading to it was carved with scenes of nature, of men and animals and plants, in celebration of the sun-god's munificence. Much of the 'originality' of Akhenaten is anticipated here, a thousand years before him, and it is interesting to see that in both these periods of the sun-cult an emphasis is placed upon naturalism. The tombs of the nobles of the Fifth Dynasty are much bigger than those of the Fourth and of a markedly *secular* character. No gods intrude upon the scenes of everyday life recorded here, and pharaoh is given his due in inscriptions without ever being shown. In fact, not even the noble owners of these tombs are much in- volved in the friezes of varied life on their walls: rather the noble sits passively watching life go on, apparently content simply that it should be so. And the cameos of everyday life that stand frozen before the nobles' gaze stay securely within the bounds of the typical and recurrent. Fishing, looking after the herds, growing corn, catching birds, bringing offerings to the tomb, writing up the accounts, working at the crafts, dancing, making bread and beer—the men and women of the nobles' estates are recorded about their daily affairs in an unchanging world of nature. No special events of the life-time of the deceased are immortalized, no promises of transfiguration in heaven are sketched out. We could not be further from the Christian next-world, of reward and punishment and bliss through some unimaginable alteration of existence away from life on earth. In fact these Egyptian dead did not go to live in a next-world at all, they continued to enjoy this one. They enjoyed its typical com- ponents, the things that are of this world, the things that are eternal not because they run on continuously but because they continually recur. At the end of the Old Kingdom, the nobles' tombs reached great heights of elaboration, like Mereruka's with his giant statue, as the central power of the king declined.

In the social collapse of the First Intermediate Period, things happened which simply ought not to have been possible in the eyes of the ancient Egyptians. The old order passed away and, though central power was eventually re-asserted, men knew that things could never be quite the same again. They had seen the world turned upside down: 'Gold and silver and turquoise . . . hang round the necks of servant girls. Noble ladies wander through the land, and mistresses of houses say "if only we had something to eat"'. The Egyptians came as close as they would ever come to the sentiments of Shakespeare's sixty-fourth sonnet as a result of this upheaval: 'The gods and those who rest in their pyramids . . . they built their temples, but their places are gone . . . I have heard the sayings of Imhotep and Hardedef, which are so much repeated, where are their places now? Their walls are demolished and they are gone as if they had never been'. Shakespeare sadly faced the fact that his image of change and decay and loss correctly 'fitted the universe he inhabited, but the Egyptians' sense of a divine order of things was much more deeply ingrained and they never lost their sense of outrage and bewilderment that such upsets could be. The pharaohs of the Middle Kingdom might establish their powers anew, but the mere fact that they had needed to be re-established altered men's attitude to them.

Chapter X Egyptian Religion and Morality

When the central authority of the Egyptian kings was first re-asserted at the dawn of the Middle Kingdom by some princes of Upper Egypt, a style of rigid austerity was applied to their mortuary statues. The figure of king Mentuhotep Nebhepetre, whose power finally embraced the whole land, displays this style today in the Cairo Museum. He was the king whose rock-cut tomb at Deir el-Bahri was fronted by a mortuary temple with a mastaba-like, truncated pyramid on top: an indication of his intent to assume the mantle of the Old Kingdom rulers. The close of the First Intermediate Period and the Middle Kingdom see an apparent change in one of the provisions of the tomb: instead of relying on carved and painted wall-scenes to invoke the eternal world of the living dead, wooden models (sometimes other materials were used) seem to have been introduced in great numbers at this time. It does not appear to be simply a case of increased survival of these models over Old Kingdom finds, but an actual resort to models to 'flesh out' the images of life in the tomb. Perhaps some more crudely magical expression of the idea of taking one's servants with one into the after-life was here at work among the newly elevated nobility of the day. At all events, the results whilst blessed with a certain naïve charm mark a decline in artistic achievement: there are models of houses and household staff like brewers and butchers, and there are a great many boats of all sorts, both luxury and work-a-day, which were interestingly orientated with the river in the tombs, sailing boats to the south and rowing boats to the north.

With the Middle Kingdom rulers, the paradox of the union of the man with the role was now favouritely expressed in the image of the sphinx, where the body of a lion with the force of royal symbolism was topped by the human head of the individual ruler. The Egyptians were always technically very proficient at combining the attributes of the animal world and the human: many of their gods are represented in this form, with animal heads on a human body unlike the sphinxes, but always with a 'seamless join'. A contrast seems to have developed in Middle Kingdom art between the realistic portrayal of the rulers, like Sesostris III whose statues show him manfully shouldering the burdens of the divine kingship, and the depiction of officials (and women) where a rather bland and featureless stylization came over the work that loses both the transient portraiture and the metaphysical idealization of the best Old Kingdom pieces. One such example is the statue of the official Chertihotep; interestingly enough his is the sort of face that has often been chosen by the popular cinema to represent Egyptian-ness!

From the Middle Kingdom comes a quantity of jewellery, like the pectorals (to hang across the chest) of Sesostris II and III or Ammenemes III, and the crown of princess Sit-Hathor-Yunet. These pieces rival or better the more famous jewels of Tutankahmun.

Of the Hyksos rule there are little or no monuments at all, but we may be sure that the social upheaval of their times must have re-inforced the melancholy strain that entered Egyptian thought as a result of the First Intermediate Period. When the dynasties of the New Kingdom gained possession of the land and re-imposed the rule of the native pharaohs, the role of the king had changed once more and consequently the artistic depiction of these rulers was altered. These were kings used to proving themselves in battle, not only inside Egypt, but also against the foreign enemies of the empire. Concrete deeds could now be more fully celebrated and temple walls of New Kingdom times were decorated with huge renderings of battles and conquests: the styles employed were still the old eternal and idealized ones, but they were certainly being applied to new forms. And interestingly, the personal role of particular pharaohs in conferring honours and advancement was recognized in depicting the king in person in the wall-scenes of the nobles' tombs: an unheard-of feature in Old Kingdom times. From being a remote and cosmically endowed god-king, pharaoh had become to some extent a secular source of preferment.

The terraced temple of Hatshepsut at Deir el-Bahri is not only important because it contains an authoritative statement of the notion of the 'divine birth of pharaoh', showing the fathering of the future queen upon her mother by Amun-Re, but also because it is a supreme instance of the Egyptians' gift for placing their architectural creations in perfect accord with their natural surroundings. The vast natural amphitheatre of reddish cliffs against which the three ascending terraces of simple colonnades are set has been selected with great sureness of eye as a positively cosmic setting for Hatshepsut's mortuary temple. The same sensitivity to matters of architectural integration with environment is seen in the Giza group of pyramids and the great Sphinx carved out of living rock on the desert's edge above old Memphis, and in the vast temples of Abu Simbel

Previous page *A sternly noble statue of Ammenemes IV displays the strength of character of the Twelfth Dynasty rulers.*

Above *This Middle Kingdom statue, of an official named Chertihotep, reveals a degree of blandness that too many have taken for an image of all Egyptian art.*

Left *Mentuhotep was the prince of Thebes who consolidated the Middle Kingdom after a period of social discord.*

cut in the barren hillside of the far south. Hatshepsut's temple lies a long way from her tomb, which is in the Valley of the Kings, and this pattern of a separation of secreted tomb and manifest mortuary temple was maintained by all the New Kingdom rulers. The temple was thus kept close to the living, perhaps closer than ever before and actually in the fields of the river plain, while the tomb itself was tucked away in the barren Theban Hills, out of sight and out of reach of robbers.

The tombs of the nobles of this period, while superficially repeating (in paint where the former ones had been carved too) the themes of the Old Kingdom tombs, show many changes and even some experimental traits. The nobles are no longer depicted in that detached and passive fashion, watching the world go by, but are much more frequently shown actually in the thick of things—themselves hunting and fishing and in one case driving a chariot. Evidently the vision of eternity and what was valuable in it had shifted towards personal ends rather than the general celebration of a whole spectrum of typical recurrences. This is in keeping with the social conditions of New Kingdom times, when imperial conquest and wealth and trade had created new tastes and new ambitions among new classes. Artistic novelties were also in evidence: fragments of wall-paintings from an 'unknown tomb' in the British Museum include an attempt at a full-face portrayal of a musician at a feast.

The religious revolution master-minded by Akhenaten cannot now be attributed to any particular cause: it may have grown out of political considerations to do with curbing the civil power of the Amun priesthood; or it may have been owed in part at least to some dottiness of the king brought on by glandular malfunction; Nefertiti may have played this or that or no part in fostering it. It was not really as unique a departure as it has sometimes been made out to have been, since even in Old Kingdom times the cult of the sun-god had sometimes led to similar attitudes and artistic expressions. What was unique about it was its uncharacteristic and un-Egyptian intolerance of all other gods save the Aten sun-disk and the peculiarity for Egypt of this concept of divinity in itself. For the Aten disk was an absolutely manifest and revealed god with none of the immanent qualities frequently displayed by previous Egyptian deities. Amun, for instance, associated with the wind, was called the 'Hidden One' and his powers, like those of others of the gods, ran through the workings of the natural world in a pantheistic fashion. Akhenaten's god was not an immanent force but an absolutely distinct entity. Moreover, Akhenaten's exclusivity cut out the Osirian cycle of beliefs about life after death (there is not much to suggest that Akhenaten took any great interest in that), and altered the relationship of pharaoh and god. In line with the habits of prophetic souls the world over, Akhenaten put himself forward on a new footing of pre-eminence by making himself the exclusive avenue to his new deity. The rest of the Egyptian people were to approach this god only at the direction of Akhenaten himself, whereas the old gods had offered more scope and variety of appeal to the populace. In effect, Akhenaten alone dealt with his god; his people dealt through him. We may be almost sure that Akhenaten's innovations held little or no attraction for the Egyptian people as a whole, court-centred and lacking in popular mystery as these novelties were. The dedication of even Akhenaten's high-ranking courtiers is open to doubt—though they are fulsome in their references to Akhenaten in their tombs ('the god who made me' says one of them, in an unmonotheistic spirit). Some of his closest officers piloted the return to orthodoxy after his death, among them Ay who was for a short time pharaoh after Tutankhamun (Akhenaten's immediate successor) and Horemheb, the generalissimo who wrecked Akhenaten's works in the next reign.

Akhenaten's great bequest to the world is his 'Hymn to the Sun' which poetically expresses the quality of his sun-disk devotion: 'Worship . . . *the Living Aten*, the Great one in Jubilee, Master of all that the Aten encircles . . . and the King of Upper and Lower Egypt, the one Living by Maat . . . *Akhenaten*; and the First Wife of the King . . . *Nefertiti* . . .' At the very beginning, the exaltation of Akhenaten and his wife is emphasized practically on a par with the Aten's. And the hymn continues: 'You rise in perfection upon the horizon, living Aten, beginner of life . . . When you dispel darkness and send forth your rays, the Two Lands rejoice, awake and standing on their feet, now that you have raised them up . . . The entire land performs its labours: all the cattle are content with their fodder, trees and plants grow, birds fly up to their nests . . . the fish in the river leap before your face when your rays reach the waters. You have put seed in woman and made sperm in man . . . You are the nurse in the womb, giving breath to nurture all that has been conceived . . . sole god, without another beside you, you made the earth according to your desire when you were by yourself . . . You are my desire, and there is no other who knows you, except for your son Akhenaten, for you have acquainted him with your designs and your power'. What is extraordinary about these sentiments in an Egyptian context, apart from their assertion of exclusivity both for the god and his son, is not that they are expressed at all (something like them was always present in Egyptian religion) but that they are expressed to the total neglect of the other aspects of immanent divinity and concern with life-after-death that meant so much to the Egyptian religious consciousness.

'Living by Maat' is the clue to the artistic attitudes of the Amarna heresy. 'Maat', that no precisely translatable concept of truth, rectitude, good order and righteousness, that was sometimes personified as a goddess even in Akhenaten's time, was a very central concern of the heretic pharaoh, though he interpreted it in a peculiar way. Addiction to 'truthfulness' seems to have inspired Akhenaten to foster a style of so-called naturalistic art which began with portraying the pharaoh himself as a monstrosity (we can only assume he looked something like his statues in real life), went on to achieve wondrously beautiful studies of Nefertiti and other Amarna royal ladies and was perfectly realized in wall-paintings of scenes of nature of great freshness and vitality. Actually the Amarna style is as stylized as any other mode of Egyptian art; the fact is that, whilst it is based on naturalism, a new ideal has been stamped upon it, in keeping with Akhenaten's particular notion of 'Maat'. 'Maat', with its many shades of meaning, was ever-important to the Egyptians and always, perhaps, carried a sense of what the world *should* be rather than what it was in practice: no one could mistake Akhenaten's application of 'Maat' for neutral and objective recording of fact (too much exaggeration and distortion is apparent in almost all Amarna art); rather he was elaborating a vision of what the world had ideally become for him.

The heretic's religious notions passed away with his rule and his artistic revolution evaporated too, though traces of its stylistic superficialities lingered for a while—for example in some of the items from Tutankhamun's tomb, like the throne-back that shows a somewhat pot-bellied king tended by his wife under the rays of the Aten sun-disk (some of these objects may even be thought to have belonged in the first place to Akhenaten).

The new dynasty of the Ramessides, in keeping with their military vigour and imperial posture, returned in full to the broad artistic and religious fold of their pre-Amarna forbears, only writ blatantly large. Champollion once remarked of Egyptian architecture: 'their conceptions are those of men a hundred feet high'. This certainly suits the work of Ramesses II, who built on a massive scale. His great rock-cut temple at Abu Simbel in the far south, which was recently rescued from the waters of lake Nasser, is a most impressive instance of the manipulation of nature for effect: the natural setting is magnificently exploited and the depths of the temple are orientated so that at the right time the rays of the morning sun can penetrate to the far end of the shrine and light up the figures of the gods perhaps in an image of the daily rebirth of the world and the conquest of darkness and death. Elsewhere among Ramesses II's enterprises, a note of disproportion and exaggeration is unmistakable: the Hypostyle Hall at Karnak approaches a crowded and clumsy hyperbole. Colossal statuary, like the great figure of Ramesses II that now lies among the ruins of old Memphis, was the order of the day: the paradoxical theme of divine royalty is here handled in terms of the imposingly large. Probably more stone was quarried and shipped and fashioned at this time than went into the building of the pyramids!

By contrast with the monumental gestures of the pharaohs of the Nineteenth and Twentieth Dynasties, the modest Theban tombs of artists and craftsmen at Deir el-Medina bear witness on a human scale to the lives and attitudes of the more ordinary Egyptians of this time. What is striking about them is the changeover from scenes celebrating daily life in the manner of the Eighteenth Dynasty nobles' tombs (or of the Old Kingdom tombs) to an emphasis upon depictions of embalming, rituals of the tomb, offerings, images of the bird-headed 'ba'-soul and so forth. The same morbid drift is manifest in the royal tombs of these dynasties, even more elaborately: with great concentration upon mythological elements, spells, renderings of the 'Book of the Dead', details of the journey of the soul in the after-life. The progressive loss of Egyptian power and influence in late New Kingdom times, and the tensions of the social scene at home, are matched in terms of religious art by a clear decline in confidence in life and after-life, a growing reliance on mumbo-jumbo and a morbid concern with the minutiae of survival in the next world. Finally all art vanished from the tombs of the Egyptian citizenry after the Twentieth Dynasty and efforts were concentrated upon the decoration of the coffin alone, which was painted with magico-religious symbols and spells. A pre-occupation with the myth and ritual of the resurrection-god and ruler of the underworld, Osiris, marks this time. The native Egyptian tradition enjoyed another flowering, however, in the period of the Saïtes, after about 660 BC when trade with Greece created a new prosperity and native Egyptian rulers were able to hold power until defeated at the hands of the Persians in 525 BC. The Ethiopian rulers who preceded the Saïte Twenty-sixth Dynasty had modelled themselves and their art upon the Old Kingdom and Middle Kingdom examples and the Saïtes, along the same lines, achieved some remarkably impressive results. They were not, of course, able to resurrect the classical expression of the Old Kingdom, but works like the statue of the viceroy Mentuemhet in the Cairo Museum do bear comparison with the art of former days and constitute a link with the development of classical art in Greece.

Afterwards, while temples like Philae continue to impress, there came a great decadence over Egyptian art in parallel with an appalling religious decline. The frequently ugly carving of temple reliefs from Ptolemaic times and the pointless elaboration and crowding of the hieroglyphic inscriptions are matched by the development of an Egyptian mania for animal cults that took the Greeks aback and scandalized the Romans. 'I worship only gods, not cattle', said Octavian in Egypt and Juvenal asked: 'Who does not know . . . what monsters are revered by demented Egypt?' Osiris was conflated with the Apis bull of Memphis into a new deity, Serapis and, at Sakkara, the sacred bulls were buried in great underground tombs—Mariette found these bull-burials at the Serapaeum of Sakkara in the last century and Professor Emery of London University found similar cow-burials in the early 1970s. He also found, like others before him, prodigious underground tunnellings full of the embalmed bodies of sacred baboons, ibises, falcons and other animals. Over a million ibis

190

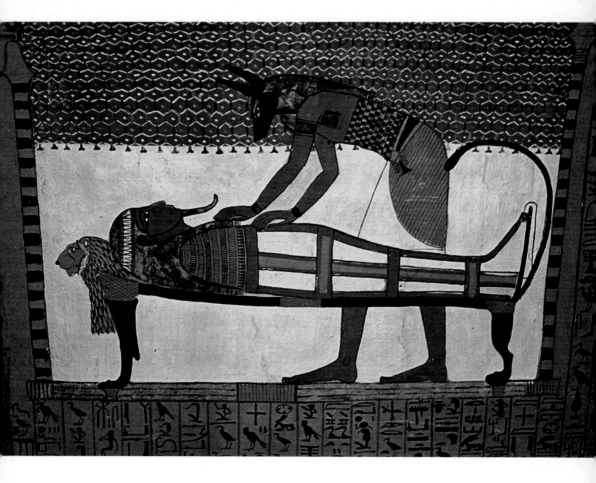

The jackal-headed Anubis, god of the graveyard, was closely identified with all aspects of death and the after-life. This painting, from a small tomb at Thebes, shows him attending to the ritual of mummification.

Next page In a relief from the tomb of Sethos I, the king receives life (in the form of the loop-handled cross or 'ankh') from the ibis-headed god Thoth whose figure well demonstrates the assurance with which the Egyptians were able to bring together human and animal attributes.

Right *In the royal tombs of the Nineteenth Dynasty, an overwhelming concern with spells and magic and the minutiae of the after-life asserts itself: here is depicted the descent of the dead man's sarcophagus into the tomb and underworld.*

Right *Among the innovations of the late New Kingdom were perspective effects that went against the former Egyptian canon, like this attempt at rendering a full-face portrayal among a group of musicians.*

Right *'Pectorals' were worn across the chest on neck-laces: from the Middle Kingdom come examples that rival the jewellery of Tutankhamun.*

Next page *The Nineteenth Dynasty, especially in the hands of Ramesses II, saw an exaggeration of scale that frequently spoils the work: the great Hypostyle Hall at Karnak is witness to this over-aggrandisement.*

193

mummies are estimated to have been located at Sakkara alone and there are similar sites elsewhere in Egypt. The latter days of ancient Egyptian religion plainly witnessed an almost insane exaggeration of a trait of that religion that distinguishes it from most others: its abiding emphasis upon animal-figured gods. The ibises and baboons may have been simply sacred animals, but we know that some such sacred animals stood in for the very gods themselves and were worshipped, whilst many of the gods throughout Egyptian history were depicted with animal attributes. The latter days of Egyptian civilization may have witnessed a shocking over-emphasis upon the animal cults, but the Egyptian religion always did find great place for gods in animal form: there were gods as wolves, hippopotamuses, falcons, toads. Some gods were an amalgam of human body and animal head, like ibis-headed Thoth, and some gods figured in both human and animal manifestations. When all is said about the origins of the many strands of Egyptian religion in separate cultural communities, living along the predynastic Nile, and when prehistoric totemism has been invoked to account for the cult of different animal gods in different places, the fact remains that throughout Egyptian history animal-figured gods co-existed with gods in human shape and won the continuing devotion of the Egyptian people. What was it about the world of nature, in particular nature's animal life, that so recommended itself to the Egyptian consciousness? An answer to this question involves the Egyptians' adherence to the idea of the eternal and the ever-recurring essentials of life. What interested them was what does not occur only once, but what recurs for ever, what does not change with time but remains eternally the same. Plainly anything that manifests these qualities that the Egyptians so esteemed must be part of the divine order of things. Whereas the generations of human beings change and change again, living very different lives, looking very different from one another, experiencing social alterations, the world of the animals does not change: tomorrow's foxes and falcons will look and behave exactly like today's and yesterday's, scarcely distinguishable as individuals, living lives that do not differ from their ancestors'. It took geologists and experimental breeders to learn that the animals also change, but at a vastly slower pace than men: the Egyptians had not encountered the bones of extinct animals or bred fruit-flies in laboratory conditions. In contrast also with the world of men, where failure and loss of confidence go hand in hand with success and assurance, the animal order gives off an aura of certainty and sure achievement: animals seem to know what they are doing, to know what they want and on the whole to get it in a way that dwarfs the everyday achievements of men. All these traits marked them off in the Egyptian mind as belonging very definitely to the realm of the divine: in that light, the animal gods of Egypt cease to appear as quaint or shocking aberrations and an obstacle to appreciating the Egyptian view of the world is removed. The Egyptians would have concurred with Walt Whitman, who observed: 'I think I could turn and live with animals, they are so placid and self-contain'd, I stand and look at them long and long'. The animal-manifestations are not primitive traits in Egyptian religion but rather ways of expressing certain attributes of divinity: the image of ibis-headed Thoth reveals this very well, for we are surely faced not with an attempt to portray an actually existing entity, but with an *ideogram* for certain aspects of the god.

By no means all the gods of Egypt had animal forms or ever figured in animal manifestations. A complete listing of the Egyptian gods is impossible for, among the lesser and more locally restricted divinities, multitudes obtain. A list of the more major deities would exceed eighty. As with the Egyptian approach to the problems of death and life after death, a number of variant religious beliefs always existed side by side and the Egyptians were glad to possess a variety of approaches towards divinity that was not impoverished by any fanatical exclusiveness (except under Akhenaten). Where the different avenues seem to be inconsistent to our eyes, the Egyptians saw no need for congruity—some of their intellectual priesthoods did strive to bring all the disparate material together and create all-embracing theologies, but even their efforts left great scope for the believers.

Though there were many gods in ancient Egypt and Egypt was itself ruled by a living god, though these gods took many and baffling forms and their roles overlapped or contradicted each other, though the cult of the gods was a vital matter of daily observance in temples up and down the land, though in short ancient Egypt might appear to have been the most religious of nations as Herodotus thought, the ethical content of Egyptian belief remained startlingly rational and unmysterious in a way that would not have shamed a Bloomsbury humanist. The moral precepts of the Egyptians make little or no appeal to divine command, though the approval of the gods in a sensible everyday way is sometimes invoked. The literature of ethical maxims and advice is considerable and most of its content would strike a modern reader as rather admirable if sometimes a bit obvious. Like the tomb pictures of the Old and Middle and New Kingdoms (until the strain of other-worldly anxiety overwhelmed them), Egyptian morality was firmly anchored in the rational concerns of everyday life and did not depend upon the unconditional commands of a god from the beyond. In keeping with its rational and humanistic character, Egyptian belief failed on the whole to develop a very full notion of evil: there is Seth, the enemy and assassin of Osiris, and there is the serpent of darkness, Apophis, with whom the sun-god daily contends; but there is certainly no Satan nor any dualism of good and evil. The Egyptians equally failed to realize a truly awesome image of their gods, who remain either very much in the human mould (if majestic) or in the nature of

196

Among the last statements of the great Egyptian artistic tradition, often consciously modelled upon the past, are the products of the Saïtes and other late Egyptian dynasties: this head of the viceroy Mentuemhet preserves something of the heritage.

ideograms for some aspect of divinity: there is nothing to compare with the images of awful godhead found in, for example, Mesopotamian or ethnographic contexts.

'Maat' is the constant component of Egyptian morality, the personified standard of truth, righteousness and good conduct by which the affairs of men were to be conducted and judged. Its application ranged from matters of worldly discretion and prudence to instances of a more disinterested sort of ethical behaviour. In a few examples selected, with admitted partiality, from a body of ethical precepts from different periods of Egyptian history, let the ancient Egyptians characterize themselves as moralists:

> 'When you grow up and take a wife and become the head of your own household, remember how your mother bore you and reared you. May she never have cause to blame you or raise her hands to God—and may God never have to hear her lament'.

> 'Love your wife in your house . . . care for her needs . . . clothe her . . . gladden her heart . . . she is a field, the tilling of which brings rewards to him who has her'.

> 'Do right as long as you live on earth; comfort the weeping, offend not the widow, deprive no man of his inheritance. Do not be angry: it is good to be friendly. The good conduct of the righteous man is more welcome than the ox sacrificed by the wrong-doer'.

> 'A man proves himself if he goes by that which is right . . . by so doing, he will gather riches, but the greedy man will remain without a tomb. The courageous man who does not give in to his whims will be master of himself and master of his affairs. The weak man who follows his fancies will reap hatred instead of love'.

> 'If a poor man owes you debts, divide them into three and give up two parts of them—you will find that such are the ways of life. To be praised as a friend of men is worth more than riches in store'.

And finally:

> 'Goodly speech is rarer than precious turquoise, yet it may be found with the servant girls at their grindstones'.

List of illustrations

LINE DRAWINGS

Page

All maps and drawings are by John McWatt, F.R.G.S.

19 Map. The principal sites of ancient Egypt.

27 Map. The headwaters of the Nile.

39 Map. The 'Fertile Crescent'.

46 The Scorpion mace-head.

Page

79 A 'serekh'.

80 The docket of Aha.

86 The sign for 'foreign country'.

97 Map. Egypt in the Ancient World.

118 Scene from a relief depicting Hatshepsut's 'divine birth'. After Pierre Montet.

125 Nome standards.

155 An obelisk raft from a relief in Hatshepsut's temple. After Naville.

BLACK AND WHITE PHOTOGRAPHS

Page

6 Brown quartzite statue of Senwosret-senebefny. Dynasty XII. Napoleon's gift to Josephine. By courtesy of the Brooklyn Museum, Charles Edwin Wilbour Fund.

9 Pompey's Pillar, Alexandria. Photo: John Ross.

11 A sketch, annotated by Napoleon, of the pyramids at Giza. Photo: Frank Leek.

11 The Great Sphinx as Napoleon's army saw it. From Vivant Denon, *Voyage dans la Basse et la Haute Egypte, pendant les campagnes du Général Bonaparte* (1802).

13 The Rosetta Stone. By courtesy of the Trustees of the British Museum.

Page

21 Surviving casing-stones at the summit of the Chephren Pyramid, Giza. Dynasty IV. Photo: Paul Jordan.

21 False door from an Old Kingdom tomb. British Museum. Photo: Paul Jordan.

29 Hippos carved in relief in the tomb of Mereruka, Sakkara. Dynasty VI. Hirmer Fotoarchiv, Munich.

30 Prehistoric rock drawings at Gerf Husain, Nubia. Photo: Cyril Aldred.

30 Gerzean painted pot. Predynastic. By courtesy of the Department of Antiquities, Ashmolean Museum.

36 Osiriform tray of sprouting corn. From Tutankhamun's tomb, Valley of the Kings. Dynasty XVIII. Cairo Museum. Photo: Griffith Institute, Ashmolean Museum.

Page

44 A crouched, desert burial. Predynastic. British Museum. Photo: Robert Harding Associates.

44 Inscribed base of a statue of Djoser. Dynasty III. Cairo Museum. Photo: John Ross.

44 Two small statues of Tutankhamun as they were found, swathed and packed in a coffer, in his tomb in the Valley of the Kings. Dynasty XVII. Cairo Museum. Photo: Griffith Institute, Ashmolean Museum.

47 The Narmer Palette. Reverse. Early Dynastic. Cairo Museum. Photo: Hirmer Fotoarchiv, Munich.

47 The mace-head of the Scorpion King. Early Dynastic. By courtesy of the Department of Antiquities, Ashmolean Museum.

48 The Narmer Palette. Obverse. Early Dynastic. Cairo Museum. Photo: Hirmer Fotoarchiv, Munich.

54 Obelisk at Kingston Lacey. From Philae. Photo: Peter Clayton.

54 Portrait of Thomas Young (1773–1829). By courtesy of the Royal Society. Photo: A. C. Cooper.

54 Portrait of Jean-François Champollion (1790–1832). By courtesy of the Louvre.

61 Toppled statue of Ramesses II, Ramesseum, Thebes. Dynasty XIX. Photo: John Ross.

61 Portrait of Giovanni Battista Belzoni (1778–1823). Photo: Peter Clayton.

64 Portrait of Auguste Ferdinand Mariette (1821–81). Photo: Mary Evans Picture Library.

64 Portrait of Mohamed Ali (1769–1849). By courtesy of the *Illustrated London News*.

64 Portrait of Sir (William Matthew) Flinders Petrie (1853–1942). By courtesy of the National Portrait Gallery.

66 Statue of Chephren. From Giza. Dynasty IV. Cairo Museum. Photo: John Ross.

82 The Palermo Stone. By courtesy of the Museo Archaeologico, Palermo.

82 Den smiting the Easterners. Ivory plaquette from Abydos. Dynasty I. By courtesy of the British Museum.

82 Statue of Djoser from Sakkara. Dynasty III. Cairo Museum. Photo: John Ross.

Page

90 The 'collapsed' pyramid of Meidum. Dynasty III. Photo: Paul Jordan.

90 The mummy of Nefer. From Sakkara. Dynasty IV. Photo: Paul Jordan.

91 The pyramids of Cheops, Chephren and Mycerinus at Giza. Dynasty IV. Photo: John Ross.

92 Ti hunting hippos from a boat. Relief from his tomb at Sakkara. Dynasty V. Photo: Hirmer Fotoarchiv, Munich.

92 Ptolemaic reliefs from the temple at Kom Ombo. Photo: John Ross.

92 Magical texts inscribed on the wall of the pyramid of Wenis, Sakkara. Dynasty V. Photo: John Ross.

102 Statue of Sesostris III. From Deir el-Bahri. Dynasty XII. Cairo Museum. Photo: Hirmer Fotoarchiv, Munich.

102 Temple of Hatshepsut, Deir el-Bahri. Dynasty XVIII. Photo: John Ross.

102 The queen of Punt. Relief from the temple of Hatshepsut, Deir el-Bahri. Dynasty XVIII. Photo: John Ross.

109 Chariot. From the tomb of Tutankhamun, Valley of the Kings. Dynasty XVIII. Cairo Museum. Photo: Griffith Institute, Ashmolean Museum.

109 Statue of Akhenaten. Dynasty XVIII. Louvre. Photo: John Ross.

109 Head of queen Tiy. Inlaid ebony. Dynasty XVIII. By courtesy of the Egyptian Museum, Berlin.

110 Head of Nefertiti. Brown quartzite. From Amarna. Dynasty XVIII. Cairo Museum. Photo: John Ross.

120 Tuthmosis III smiting the Easterners. Relief at Karnak. Dynasty XVIII. Photo: A. A. M. van der Heyden.

120 Prince Ankhhaf. Limestone bust, faced with stucco. Dynasty IV. By courtesy of the Museum of Fine Arts, Boston.

127 A company of soldiers. Wooden tomb model from Asyut. Dynasty X. Cairo Museum. Photo: John Ross.

127 Military trumpets. From the tomb of Tutankhamun, Valley of the Kings. Dynasty XVIII. Photo: Griffith Institute, Ashmolean Museum.

128 Seated scribe. Painted limestone statue. From Sakkara. Dynasty V. By courtesy of the Louvre.

Page

128 A scribe's writing kit. From the tomb of Tutankhamun, Valley of the Kings. Cairo Museum. Photo: Griffith Institute, Ashmolean Museum.

130 Tutankhamun wearing the red crown of the North and carrying the royal insignia. Gilded wooden statue from his tomb, Valley of the Kings. Dynasty XVIII. Cairo Museum. Photo: Griffith Institute, Ashmolean Museum.

130 Scribes. Limestone relief. By courtesy of the Soprintendenza alle Antichita dell' Etruria, Florence.

136 Return of the herds. Painted limestone relief from the tomb of Ti, Sakkara. Dynasty V. Photo: Hirmer Fotoarchiv, Munich.

136 Wine-making. Copy by Nina de Garis Davies of a wall-painting from the tomb of Khaemueset, Thebes. Dynasty XVIII. By courtesy of the Trustees of the British Museum.

139 Sarcophagus of queen Meresankh. From Giza. Dynasty IV. Photo: Peter Clayton.

139 A granary. Wooden tomb model from Beni Hasan. Dynasties IX–XII. By courtesy of the Department of Antiquities, Ashmolean Museum.

143 Priest in leopard-skin robe. Wall-painting from the tomb of Tutankhamun, Valley of the Kings. Dynasty XVIII. Photo: Griffith Institute, Ashmolean Museum.

143 Prince Rahotep and his wife Nofret. Painted limestone statue. From Meidum. Dynasty IV. Cairo Museum.

143 The sandalled feet of Tutankhamun. From his tomb in the Valley of the Kings. Dynasty XVIII. Cairo Museum. Photo: Griffith Institute, Ashmolean Museum.

148 The Fields of Yalu. Wall-painting from the tomb of Sennedjem, Deir el-Medina. Dynasty XIX. Photo: John Ross.

149 Isis nursing Horus. Bronze statuette. Dynasties XXI–XXXI. By courtesy of the Department of Antiquities, Ashmolean Museum.

149 The Ba, part of the soul represented as a bird. Wall-painting from the tomb of Arinefer, Thebes. Dynasty XX. © G. Nagel, Geneva.

149 Osiris as a body sprouting corn. From the Jumhilac Papyrus. Ptolemaic Period. Louvre.

Page

153 Cheops' boat. Model of the boat found in a pit near the Great Pyramid, Giza. Dynasty IV. Photo: John Ross.

153 Metalworkers. Wall-painting from the tomb of Rekhmire, Thebes. Dynasty XVIII. Photo: Robert Harding Associates.

153 A shaduf. Wall-painting from the tomb of Ipuy, Thebes. Dynasty XIX. Photo: Elsevier.

159 Ruins of the original building ramp against the first pylon at Karnak. Dynasty XXV. Photo: John Ross.

161 The zodiac of Dendera. Ptolemaic relief. By courtesy of the Louvre.

161 Hippopotamus. Faïence. New Kingdom. By courtesy of the Trustees of the British Museum.

162 Cleopatra's Needle encased in a cylinder ready to be towed from Alexandria to London. By courtesy of the Museum of London.

162 A half-finished obelisk at Aswan. By courtesy of Edizione l'Elefante, Rome.

162 Hatshepsut's obelisk, Karnak. Dynasty XVIII. Photo: Robert Harding Associates.

167 Swimming girl. The carved, wooden handle of a cosmetic spoon. New Kingdom. Cairo Museum. Photo: John Ross.

Mice as masters. Satirical drawing on papyrus. Dynasty XIX. Cairo Museum.

167 The phoenix-heron. Papyrus drawing. By courtesy of the Trustees of the British Museum.

167 Ptah. Bronze statuette. By courtesy of the Department of Antiquities, Ashmolean Museum.

171 Stuccoed, wooden chest, painted with a battle scene. From the tomb of Tutankhamun, Valley of the Kings. Dynasty XVIII. Cairo Museum. Photo: Griffith Institute, Ashmolean Museum.

171 Ka statue of Hor. From Dashur. Dynasty XII. Cairo Museum. Photo: Hirmer Fotoarchiv, Munich.

171 The Oxford Palette. From Hieraconpolis. Predynastic. By courtesy of the Department of Antiquities, Ashmolean Museum.

176 Geese. Painted frieze from the tomb of Nefermat, Meidum. Dynasty IV. Cairo Museum.

176 Ivory statuette of a king. From Abydos. Predynastic. By courtesy of the Trustees of the British Museum.

Page

176 Mycerinus standing between two goddesses. Green slate statue from his temple
at Giza. Cairo Museum. Photo: John Ross.

179 Djoser running the ceremonial race. Relief
from his tomb at Sakkara. Dynasty III.
Photo: John Ross.

180 Mereruka. Giant statue in his tomb at
Sakkara. Dynasty VI. Photo: John Ross.

185 Ammenemes IV. Stone head. Dynasty XII.
Photo: John Ross.

186 Mentuhotep Nebhepetre. Painted sandstone statue from his temple at Deir
el-Bahri. Dynasty XI. Photo: John Ross.

186 Chertihotep. Sandstone statue. From near
Asyut. Egyptian Museum, Berlin.

Page

193 The descent into the underworld. Wall-
painting from the tomb of Ramesses VI,
Valley of the Kings. Photo: Peter Clayton.

193 Musicians at a feast. Wall-painting from
an unknown tomb at Thebes. Dynasty
XVIII. British Museum.

193 Pectoral of Sesostris III. From Lisht.
Dynasty XII. Photo: John Ross.

194 The Hypostyle Hall, Karnak. Photo:
A. A. M. van der Heyden.

197 Mentuemhet. Granite statue. Dynasty XXV.
Cairo Museum.

COLOUR PHOTOGRAPHS

Page

33 The black soil of the Nile's banks. Photo:
Robin Constable.

34 The Step Pyramid complex of Djoser,
Sakkara. Dynasty III. Photo: John Ross.

51 Ivory statuette of Cheops. From Abydos.
Dynasty IV. Cairo Museum. Photo: John
Ross.

52 The Grand Gallery of the Great Pyramid
of Cheops, Giza. Dynasty IV. Photo: John
Ross.

69 Wooden statue of Ka-aper (Sheikh-el-
Beled, or the Village Headman). From
Sakkara. Dynasty V. Cairo Museum.
Photo: John Ross.

70 Hesi-re. Wooden relief from his tomb at
Sakkara. Dynasty III. Cairo Museum.
Photo: John Ross.

87 Gilt furniture from the tomb of queen
Hetepheres, Giza. Dynasty IV. Cairo
Museum. Photo: John Ross.

88 Gold and obsidian head of a falcon. From
Hieraconpolis. Dynasty VI. Cairo Museum.
Photo: Peter Clayton.

Page

105 A noble's daughters. Painted relief from
an unknown tomb at Thebes. Dynasty XII.
Photo: John Ross.

106 Tutankhamun's gold coffin. From his
tomb in the Valley of the Kings. Dynasty
XVIII. Cairo Museum. Photo: Hirmer
Fotoarchiv, Munich.

123 Necklace of gold flies. From the tomb of
queen Aahotep, Valley of the Kings.
Dynasty XVII. Photo: Albert Shoucaire.

124 Columns of the Hypostyle Hall at Karnak.
Dynasty XIX. Photo: Sarah Tyzack.

173 A duck flying out of the reeds. Wall-
painting from Amarna. Dynasty XVIII.
Photo: John Ross.

174 A girl acrobat painted on a limestone
ostracon. Dynasty XVIII. Turin Museum.
Photo: John Ross.

191 The god Anubis preparing a body for
burial. Wall-painting from the tomb of
Sennedjem, Deir el-Medina. Dynasty XX.
Photo: A. A. M. van der Heyden.

192 Painted relief from the tomb of Sethos I,
Valley of the Kings. Dynasty XIX. Photo:
John Ross.

Index

Page numbers in italic refer to illustrations and their captions

Aahotep, 100, 154; *123*
Abdel Latif, 22
Abu Haggag, 115
Abu Simbel, 57, 67, 108, 184–7, 189
Abukir, Battle of, 10
Abusir, 93, 181
Abydos, 86, 177; *51, 176*; excavations at, 67, 71; mace-heads, 43, 45; pottery, 42–3, 79; tombs, 80, 81, 83
Africanus, 76
After-life, belief in, 135–7, 142–50; *148*
Agriculture, development of, 31–8, 40, 41, 137–8
Aha, 79, 80; *80*
Åkerblad, Johann David, 53, 57
'Akh', 144
Akhenaten, 76, 104–8, 111, 116, 121, 126, 140, 144, 172, 181, 187–9, 196; *109*
Akkadians, 95–6, 99; cuneiform, 103, 131
Alexander the Great, 53, 57, 75, 114, 134
Alexandria, 8, 14–15, 53, 65–7, 76, 114; Pompey's Pillar, 8; *9*
Ali Kosh, 37
Amarna, 107, 111, 140, 172, 178; 'Amarna' style, 107, 189; *109, 173*; tablets, 103, 104, 112
Amasis, 114
Amélineau, abbé, 71, 80
Amenophis I, 77
Amenophis III, 17, 67, 103–4, 108
American Academy of Arts, 16
Ammenemes I, 78, 98
Ammenemes III, 98, 184
Ammenemes IV, *185*
Amosis, 100
Amun, 100, 104, 107, 111, 112, 115, 117, 119, 187
Amun-Re, 184
Anatolia, 37, 108, 154
Animals, cults of, 190–6; domestication, 37, 38, 41
'Ankh', 142, *143*
Ankhesenamun, 108
Ankhhaf, 122, 178; *120*
Anubis, *191*
Apis, 190
Apophis, 99, 196
Apries, 114
Arabs, conquest of Egypt, 20–2, 115

Archaeology, development of, in Egypt, 59–73
Archaic Period, 78–83, 177
Armant, 12
Art, 169–81, 183–7; 'Amarna' style, 107, 189; *109*; Middle Kingdom, *105*; New Kingdom, *193*; Old Kingdom, 93; *92*; Saïte Dynasty, 190; *197*; *see also* Statues; Tomb-paintings
Assyrians, 68, 113
Astronomy, 122, 151–2, 163, 164
Aswan, 32, 101, 152, 155, 156; *162*; High Dam, 28, 31, 32
Asyut, 32
Atbara, river, 26–7
Aten sun-disk cult, 104, 107, 187, 188, 189
Atum, 147, 166, 168
Augustus, Emperor, 115
Australopithecines, 28
Avaris, 99, 111
Ay, 108, 188; *143*

'Ba', 144, 148
Babylonians, 113, 164
Bankes, William, 63
Baumgarten, Martin, 23
Behistun, 68
Belzoni, Giovanni Battista, 60–3; *61*
Bent Pyramid, 85
Bible, 16–17, 35, 101
Blue Nile, river, 26–7
Boats, 152; *153*; obelisks transported by, 156; *155*
'Book of the Dead', 150, 190
Boston Museum, 141
Bouchard, Pierre, 12
British Museum, 16, 24–5, 62, 65, 81, 86, 177, 187
Brooklyn Museum, 14, 132
Bruce, James, 24, 50
Brugsch, Karl Heinrich, 59
Bubastis, 114
Bull-burials, 67, 190
Burials, Neolithic, 41
Byblos, 42, 81, 86, 96, 112

Cairo, 8, 17, 22, 41, 65–7
Cairo Museum, 86, 100, 104, 107, 108, 141, 158, 172, 177, 183, 190
Cairo Opera House, 67–8

Calendar, 77–8, 151
Cambyses, 114
Carchemish, 113
Champollion, Jean-François, 16, 23, 53, 55–9, 63, 76, 160, 189; *54*
Chariots, 100; *109*
Cheops, 75, 85, 86, 121, 122, 178; *51, 120; see also* Giza, Great Pyramid
Chephren, 67, 122, 178; *66; see also* Giza, Chephren Pyramid
Chertihotep, 184; *186*
Christianity, 115
Chronology: Egyptian, 75–8; Mesopotamian, 95
Clarke, Daniel, 15
Climate, 26–31, 140
Clothing, 141–2; *143*
'Colossi of Memnon', 17–18, 103–4
'Commission of Arts and Science', 8, 10, 12, 14–15, 16
Constantinople, 22
Coptic Church, 23
Coptic language, 23, 53, 57–8, 59, 160
Creation-myths, 165–8; *167*
Crete, 98
Cults: of animals, 190–6; Aten sun-disk, 104, 107, 187, 188, 189; *see also* Religion
Cyprus, 38

Dacier, M., 57
Darwin, Charles, 71
Dashur, 85, 86, 98
Dating techniques, 'sequence dating', 72
'Decree of Canopus', 58
Deir el-Bahri, 96–7, 100, 101, 119, 183, 184
Deir el-Medina, 133, 135, 172, 189–90
Den, 81; *82*
Dendera, 12, 164; *161*
Denon, Vivant, 8, 12, 16
Diet, 138
Diodorus Siculus, 62
Diseases, detected in mummies, 140; *see also* Medicine
Djer, 81
Djoser, 49, 122, 177, 178; *44, 82; see also* Sakkara, Step Pyramid
Drovetti, Bernardino, 63, 76
Dynasties: First, 78, 80; Second, 78, 80, 81, 83; Third, 81, 83–5, 177; Fourth, 81, 85–9, 93, 178; Fifth, 83, 89–93, 178–81; Sixth, 93–4, 95, 96; Seventh, 95; Eighth, 95; Ninth, 95; Tenth, 95; Eleventh, 78, 96–7; Twelfth, 78, 97–8; Thirteenth, 98, 99; Fourteenth, 99; Fifteenth, 99; Sixteenth, 99; Seventeenth, 100; Eighteenth, 101–8, 126; Nineteenth, 108–11, 112, 126; Twentieth, 111, 112; Twenty-first, 112; Twenty-second, 112; Twenty-third, 113; Twenty-fourth, 113; Twenty-fifth, 113; Twenty-sixth, 113–14; Twenty-seventh, 114; Twenty-eighth, 114; Twenty-ninth, 114; Thirtieth, 114

Edfu, 20, 67, 114
Egypt Exploration Fund, 68
'Egyptian faïence', 42, 158
Elam, 113
Elgin, Lord, 15
El-Lahun, 98
Emery, W. B., 80, 89, 190

Encyclopaedists, 7
Erman, Johann Peter Adolf, 59, 68
Ethiopia, 26, 27, 113, 138, 190
Eusebius, 76

Fayum, 28–31, 41, 42, 43, 98, 152
Fellaheen, 117, 129, 132–3
'Fertile Crescent', 31–2, 37; *39*
First Intermediate Period, 78, 95–6
Fort Julien, 12
Fourier, J.B.J., 15, 55
France: antiquarian explorations, 24; occupation of Egypt, 7–15
Furniture, 85–6, 155; *87*

Ganj Dareh, 37
Gardiner, Alan, 59
Gibraltar, Ishmael, 60
Giza, 40, 63–5, 89, 155, 156, 178, 184; *11, 88, 91*; Chephren Pyramid, 22, 67, 89, 98, 145, 156; *21*; Great Pyramid of Cheops, 17, 20, 22, 23, 68, 84, 85, 86, 145, 152, 157; *52*
Gliddon, George, 63
Gold-work, 154; *88, 106, 123*
Great Britain: antiquarian explorations, 24; gains control of Egypt, 14–15
Great Pyramid of Cheops, *see* Giza
Greaves, John, 23
Greece: art, 169, 175, 190; conquest of Egypt, 114–15; development of agriculture, 38; idea of after-life, 145; scientific thought, 157, 165; trade with Egypt, 113, 114, 190

Hamilton, William, 15
Hardedef, 182
Harun al-Rashid, 20
Hathor, 45, 119
Hatshepsut, 97, 101, 119, 133, 152, 156, 164, 184, 187; *102, 118, 155, 162*
Hawara, 18, 98
Hearst, William Randolph, 14
Heliopolis, 117, 122, 166; Battle of, 14
Hemon, 121
Heracleopolis, 95
Herihor, 111
Herodotus, 17, 26, 75, 79, 86, 98, 114, 121, 196
Hesi-re, 177; *70*
Hetepheres, 85, 155; furniture, *87*
Heyerdahl, Thor, 152
Hieraconpolis, 46–9, 154; *88*
Hieroglyphs, 12–14, 18–20, 129; *13, 92*; decipherment, 16, 23–5, 50–9, 160; development of, 43, 45–6, 49, 81, 160, 172; *see also* Writing
Hittites, 99, 108–11, 154
Homer, 17, 18, 100
Homo erectus, 28, 31
Homo sapiens, 28, 31, 35–7
Hor, 172; *171*
Horapollon, 18
Horemheb, 75, 108, 126, 188
Horse, introduction into Egypt, 100
Horus, 45, 46, 79, 146, 166; *149*
Houses, 140–1
Huni, 85
Huntingdon, Robert, 24
Hyksos, 99–100, 103, 111, 184
'Hymn to the Sun', 107, 188
Hypatia, 115

Imhotep, 84, 122, 178, 182
Imperialism, development of Egyptian, 103
Institute of Egypt, 10
Iran, 68
Iraq, 37, 68
Isis, 20, 115, 146, 147, 166; *149*
Israelites, 111

Jarmo, 37
Jebel el-Arak, 46, 172–5
Jericho, 37
Jerusalem, 112
Jewellery, 142, 184; *123, 193*
Josephine, Empress, 8, 14
Josephus, 18, 76
Josiah, King of Judea, 113
Justinian, Emperor, 20, 22
Juvenal, 190

'Ka', 144, 172; *171*
Ka-aper, 178–81; *69*
Kadesh, 103; 111, 175
Karim Shahir, 37
Karnak, 18, 20, 24, 67, 76, 101, 107, 111, 114, 119, 156, 164; *159*; Hypostyle Hall, 28, 84, 108, 189; *124, 194*
Keith, Admiral, 15
Kemose, 100
Kharga Oasis, 28
Khartum, 41
Khyan, 99
King-lists, 18, 45, 75–7, 78
Kingston Lacey obelisk, 53, 57, 63; *54*
Kircher, Athanasius, 23–4
Kléber, General, 14
Kom Ombo, *92*
Kumma, 98
Kush, 112, 113

Language: ancient Egyptian, 23, 39, 53, 59; *see also* Hieroglyphs; Coptic, 23, 53, 57–8, 59, 160; Sumerian, 95; *see also* Writing
Lapwings, as symbol of Egyptian population, 49; *44, 46, 47*
Lascaux, 37
Late Period, 113–15
Lateran obelisk, 22
Lauer, J. P., 84
Law and order, 129
Lebanon, 42, 81, 96, 152, 156
Lepsius, Karl Richard, 58, 59
Lesseps, Ferdinand de, 67
Libya, 111, 112, 125, 163
Lisht, 98
Louis XIV, 24
Louvre, 65, 132, 146
Luxor, 18, 20, 24, 41, 96, 101, 111, 115

'Maat', 107, 121, 129, 132, 188–9, 198
Mace-heads, 43–5, 46–9; *46, 47*
Mamelukes, 8
Mamun, 20
Manchester University Museum, 155
Manetho, 18, 40, 57, 74–6, 78, 95, 99, 122
Mariette, Auguste Ferdinand, 65–8, 190; *64*
Mastabas, 79, 80–1, 89, 96–7
Maspero, Gaston, 59, 68
Mathematics, 158
Medicine, 157–8

Medinet Habu, 111, 114
Megiddo, 103, 113
Meidum, 17, 85, 178; *90, 176*
Memphis, 22, 43, 80, 81, 95, 117; Apis bull, 190; creation-myths, 166–8; foundation of, 79; names, 94; Nile dammed at, 152; palace of Djoser, 141; statue of Ramesses II, 189
Menephthes, 111
Menes, 40, 41, 49, 74, 75, 76, 78–80, 81, 94, 152, 166
Menna, 129, 132
Menou, General, 15
Mentuemhet, 190; *197*
Mentuhotep Nebhepetre, 96–7, 183; *186*
Mereruka, 93, 181; *180*
Merneptah, *see* Menephthes
Mesolithic, 38
Mesopotamia, 81, 95–6, 113, 134, 164; art, 175; belief in after-life, 145; funeral sacrifices, 83; religion, 198; ziggurats, 84; *see also* Sumerians
Metal-working, 154; *153*
Metropolitan Museum, New York, 172
Middle Kingdom, 74, 78, 96–8; art, 184; clothing, 141; tombs, 183; *105*; viziers, 122; warfare, 126
Mitanni, 99, 103
Mohamed Ali, 32, 60, 63, 65; *64*
Moses, 111
'Mother of Pots', 79, 80
Mummification, 147, 157; *44, 90, 191*; of animals and birds, 190–5; mummies as source of knowledge of ancient Egypt, 138–40; mummies used by medieval apothecaries, 22–3; origins of, 41, 86–9, 144–5
Mycerinus, 63, 65, 75, 89, 178; *176*

Nakada, 71, 72, 79
Napoleon, 7–14, 16, 56; *11*
Narmer, 49, 79, 80, 175; *47*; Palette, 49, 81, 175; *47, 48*
Nasser, lake, 31, 32, 57, 189
Natufians, 37–8
Naucratis, 114
Naville, Henri, 68
Neanderthal Man, 28, 31
Nebuchadnezzar, 113, 114
Necho, 113–14, 163
Nectanebo I, 114
Nefer, 89, 147; *90*
Nefertiti, 104, 107, 108, 187, 189; *110*
Nelson, Horatio, 10
Neolithic, 38, 41–2
'Neolithic Revolution', 31, 38, 40
New Kingdom, 74, 101–13; *123*; clothing, 141–2; religion, 100; role of pharaohs, 100, 116; tombs, 42, 187; trade, 126; viziers, 122
Nietzsche, Friedrich Wilhelm, 170
Nile, river, 26–35, 38–41, 45, 98, 151; *9, 27, 39, 97*; as basis of Egyptian agriculture, 31–2, 146, 152; canal to Red Sea built, 114, 152; in creation-myths, 166; Delta, 22, 32, 35, 38, 41, 99, 111, 112; Herodotus describes, 17
Nile, Battle of the, 10
'Nilometer', 32, 152
Niuserre, 181
Nomarchs, 125
Nubayrah, 50
Nubia, 20, 31, 98, 112, 113, 125, 126, 129

Obelisks, 22, 53, 57, 63, 155–6, 164, 181; *54, 155, 162*
Octavian, 190
Old Kingdom, 74, 78, 83–94; art, 93; *92*; clothing, 141; *143*; king-lists, 45; relief carvings, 42; status of pharaohs, 116; tombs, 27, 83–5, 190; *29*; trade, 74, 125–6; warfare, 125, 126
Osiris, 24, 35, 41, 117, 146–7, 150, 166, 175, 187, 190, 196; *36, 149*
Osiris-Apis, 115
Oxford Palette, 175; *171*

Palermo Stone, 45, 76, 81, 86; *82*
Palestine, 112, 114, 163; development of agriculture, 37; Egypt aids against Assyrians, 113; Hittites threaten Egyptian interests in, 108, 111; Tuthmosis III conquers, 101–3; war with Egypt, 96
Palettes, cosmetic, 41, 42, 45, 46, 49, 175; *47, 171*
Papyrus, 131–2; boats, 152
Peking Man, 28, 31
Pepi I, *see* Phiops I
Perring, John, 63
Persia, 114, 164, 190
Petrie, William Matthew Flinders, 68–73, 77, 79, 80, 85; *64*
Pharaohs, status and role of, 39–40, 116–17, 118–22, 134
Philae, 20, 22, 53, 114, 190
Phiops I, 93, 94, 154
Phiops II, 93, 94, 95, 96
Phoenicians, 81, 96, 163
Piazzi Smyth, Charles, 68
Pithom, 111
Pitt Rivers, General, 71
Plutarch, 24
Polycrates, 114
Pottery: 'Egyptian faïence', 42, 158; from Nakada, 72; Neolithic, 41; Predynastic, 42, 43
Predynastic Period, 42–5, 71
Prehistoric period, 28–40, 41; *30*
Priesthood, role of, 117, 122; *143*
Propliopithecus, 29
Proto-Elamites, 43
Psammetichus, 113
Ptah, 94, 166–8, 175; *167*
Ptolemaic rulers, 114
Ptolemy II, 18
Ptolemy V, 14
Punt, 97, 101, 125, 152, 163; queen of *102*
Pyramid texts, 81–3, 93, 129
Pyramids, 40, 84; construction of, 155, 156–7; 'false doors', 20; *21, 180*; Fifth Dynasty, 93, 181; Fourth Dynasty, 85–6, 89; *90, 91*; French exploration of, 10; *11*; Herodotus describes, 17; Twelfth Dynasty, 97–8; *see also* Giza; Sakkara
Pyramids, Battle of the, 8

Rahotep, 141, 178; *143*
Ramesses II, 62, 76, 108–11, 175, 189; *61, 123, 193*
Ramesses III, 111, 133
Ramesses IV, 111
Ramesses XII, 111
Ramses, 111
Rawlinson, Henry Creswicke, 68
Re, 89, 104, 117, 122, 166, 168, 181
Red Sea, 114, 152, 163

Reisner, George, 85
Rekhmire, 119, 122
Religion: animal cults, 190–6; Aten sun-disk cult, 104, 107, 187, 188, 189; decline of, 190; development of, 45; and the pharaohs, 117, 118–19
Reneb, 89
Rhind, Alexander, 71
Roman Empire: idea of after-life, 145; in Egypt, 18–20, 22, 115
Rosetta, 10, 12; Stone, 12–14, 15–16, 24, 50–7, 58; *13*
Rougé, Charles de, 59

Sacy, Sylvestre de, 53, 55, 57
Sahure, 93
Said Pasha, 67
Saïs, 113
Saïte Dynasty, 113–14, 190; *197*
Sakkara, 24, 27–8, 80–1, 83, 93, 132, 137, 154, 195; Mastabat Faraun, 89; Serapeum, 65–7, 190; South Mastaba, 81, 84; Step Pyramid, 49, 81, 83–5, 113, 122, 141, 145, 177; *34, 179*
Salt, Henry, 62, 63
Samos, 114
Sanderson, John, 22–3
Sandys, George, 23
Sargon, 95
Schliemann, Heinrich, 68
Scorpion King, 49; *46, 47*
'Scribe accroupi', 132; *128*
Scribes, 129–32; *128, 130*
Sebek-hotep, 98
Sebek-nofru, 98
Second Intermediate Period, 99–100, 122–5
Sekenenre III, 100
Sekhmet, 157
Semna, 98
Sennedjem, 135
'Sequence dating', 72
Serapis, 65, 190
Serekh, 79; *79*
Sesostris I, 98
Sesostris II, 98, 184
Sesostris III, 77, 78, 98, 184; *102*
Seth, 146, 196
Sethe, 59
Sethos I, 76, 108; *192*
Seti I, *see* Sethos I
Severus, Emperor, 18
Shaduf, 152–4, 156; *153*
Shakespeare, William, 16, 23, 168, 181–2
Shelley, Percy Bysshe, 62, 111
Shepseskaf, 89
Sheshonk, 112
Sicard, Claude, 24
Sinai, 27, 37, 42, 81, 86, 96, 98, 111, 163
Sit-Hathor-Yunet, 184
Slaves, 132
Smenkhkare, 108, 140
Smith, Sir Sydney, 14, 15
Snofru, 17, 85, 86, 97
Sobat, river, 26
Society of Antiquaries, 16
Solon, 17
'The Song of the Harper', 150
Sphinx, 10, 17, 22, 23, 67, 183–4; *11*
Staan, 99

Statues, 132, 145, 177–8
Stelae, 67, 80
Step Pyramid, *see* Sakkara
Strabo, 65–7
Stukeley, William, 24
Sudan, 27, 42, 138
Sudd, 26
Suez Canal, 68
Sumer, 68, 81; art, 175; belief in the after-life, 145; development of writing, 43, 46, 95, 131, 158–60; language, 95; religion, 117; role of kings, 134; *see also* Mesopotamia
Syria, 96, 103, 108, 111, 113–14

Table of Abydos, 76, 79
Table of Sakkara, 76
Taharka, 113
'The Tale of the Eloquent Peasant', 121
Tanis, 67, 112
Taxation, 117
Teti, 93
Thebes, 95, 100, 104, 107, 133, 137, 144, 152, 172; excavations in, 12, 24, 50; 'Colossi of Memnon', 17–18; mortuary temples, 96, 101, 111; *61, 102*; tomb of Menna, 129, 132
Theodosius, Emperor, 18, 20
Thoth, 119, 168, 195, 196; *192*
Ti, 93, 132; tomb of, *29*
Timsah, lake, 114
Tiy, 107; *109*
Tomb-paintings, 135–8, 141, 142, 145, 146, 170, 183, 196; *148, 153, 191, 193*
Tomb-robbing, 17, 20, 22, 86
Tombs: Archaic Period, 80–1, 83; Deir el-Medina, 135, 172, 189–90; *148, 191*; double tombs, 80–1, 84; Eighteenth Dynasty, 190; Fifth Dynasty, 181; mastabas, 79, 80–1, 89, 96–7; Middle Kingdom, 183; *105*; New Kingdom, 42, 187; Nineteenth Dynasty, *193*; Old Kingdom, 27, 83–5, 190; *29, 180*; Predynastic Period, 43
Tools: metal, 42, 45, 154; stone, 28–31, 37, 41
Trade, 113, 114, 125–6, 190
Troy, 68, 111
Turin Canon, 76, 78–9
Turin Museum, 172
Turkey, 23, 60; Company, 23

Turner, Thomas, 15–16
Tutankhamun, 45, 104, 108, 126, 129, 134, 140 188; tomb and relics of, 24, 35, 41, 86, 142, 146, 150, 154–5, 175, 184, 189; *36, 44, 106, 109, 127, 128, 130, 143, 171*
Tuthmosis I, 101
Tuthmosis II, 101
Tuthmosis III, 76, 77, 101–3, 111; *120*

Unesco, 20
Ur, 83, 96
Userkaf, 93

Valley of the Kings, 18, 24, 84, 100, 101, 108, 132–3, 134, 135, 146, 187
Vansleb, J. B., 24
Verdi, Giuseppe, 67–8
'Village Headman', *69*
Viziers, 122
Volney, Comte de, 25
Vyse, Richard Howard, 63–5

Wadi-en-Natuf, 37
Warburton, William, 50
Warfare, 125, 126
Water-works, 152–4
Wenamun, 112
Wenis, 93, 129, 156; *92*
Wenis Pyramid, 83, 93
Wheel, use of, 100, 156
White Nile, river, 26–7
Whitman, Walt, 196
Winckelmann, Johann Joachim, 169
Wine-making, 138; *136*
Women, role of, 133–4
Writing, 129–32; *128*; Akkadian cuneiform, 103, 131; Sumerian, 43, 46, 95, 131, 158–60; *see also* Hieroglyphs

Yakub-Her, 99
Young, Thomas, 53–5, 56, 57, 58, 63; *54*

Zagros Mountains, 31, 37, 38
Zawi Chemi-Shanidar, 37
Ziggurats, 84
'Zodiac' of Dendera, 164; *161*